WIT1 __ __ __ WN

eBay For Everyone

by

Cherry Nixon

WITHDRAWN

Bernard Babani (publishing) Ltd

The Grampians

Shepherds Bush Road

London

W6 7NF

England **WITHDRAWN**

www.babanibooks.com

Please Note

Although every care has been taken with the production of this book to ensure that the information contained herewith is accurate and correct, the publishers and author do not accept responsibility in any way for any matters arising from its use. From time to time there may be changes including those of policy and fees and users need to be aware that the most current information is available on the eBay site. The views expressed are those of the author and may be at variance with the ideas of others.

First Published - May 2016

British Library Cataloguing in Publication Data.

A catalogue record for this book is available from the British Library.

ISBN 978 0 85934 760 0

Preface

This book is a guide to eBay.co.uk and the eBay App for mobile devices. The information is provided in a straightforward manner and tailored for people who have little natural aptitude with computers but are eager to access the opportunities eBay offers. It provides overviews of buying and selling followed by examples of both. It suggests a strategy for new traders and shows them how to prepare and start trading. Key concepts are explained and common problems are highlighted so that they can be avoided. It gives invaluable insight into what readily sells and how best to present items for sale. The emphasis is on safe trading. It is not a definitive work on eBay and there are many aspects of the site that have been omitted in order to present a simple route to buying and selling. It is recommended that this book is initially read in its entirety though some information is repeated to enable its use as an easy reference work. This book is more than a guide and offers ideas for getting organised and indicates the mindset for long-term successful trading. Above all else it encourages technologically untalented people to join the millions who enjoy trading on this amazing site.

Stop Press: The April 2017 trading regulations, allowing a tax free turnover of up to £1,000, means that there is no better time to start selling on eBay.

.About the Author

Cherry Nixon (BA, PGCE) is a speaker and teacher of antiques and collectables. It was whilst delivering her course at Bath University, and discussing eBay with her students, that she realised there was a need for a course on trading on the site. Fired up with purpose and enthusiasm she created the first ever hands-on course in this country. The original classes were supported by eBay UK and presented at Bath and Birmingham Universities. Since then she has taught at many venues around the country, and currently teaches and speaks on request and privately. (www.cherrypickservices.co.uk)

Trademarks

eBay.co.uk, eBay.com and PayPal are trademarks or registered trademarks of their respective companies. All other trademarks are the registered and legally protected trademarks of the companies who make the products. There is no intent to use the trademark generically moreover, readers should investigate ownership of a trademark before using it for any purpose.

Illustrations

Illustrations by Rob Page

www.robpageillustration.com

Acknowledgements

Tallulah Speed

James Peacock

Ron Speed

Contents

Introduction to eBay

Origins and Ethos

When AuctionWeb (later renamed eBay) first appeared in 1995 it was basic and straightforward. You could put an item up for auction or you could place a bid.

Twenty years on it's totally transformed. The site is packed with features and in terms of trading options you are spoilt for choice. For instance, you can bid in an Auction, Make an Offer for an item or cut out the wait and Buy it Now. Alternatively, you can head for the eBay shops, or click on to the deals of the day – and similarly on the other side of the fence are the corresponding routes for selling. The site that originally offered just a handful of categories now has several thousand sub-categories with a wide range of goods and services from vintage hosiery to fencing panels.

The result of all this change is that eBay is no longer straightforward – it's complicated. This book cuts through the complexity and reveals an easy route for newcomers. It consists of an overview of the site followed by a step-by-step guide. It also contains an easy guide to the eBay App.

However before embarking on the learning curve you need to understand how it came about. The account of the origins of eBay will inform you of the eBay ethos and afford you the best possible mindset for long-term successful trading.

eBay Changed the Commercial World

If the story of the creation of eBay were not true it would be dismissed as implausible! On the day of its launch, Labor Day 1995, AuctionWeb, (the original name) received not one visitor. However, this changed speedily and spectacularly and within a few years it had become far more than a successful site. Within a decade of its introduction it was labelled the most significant commercial development of the twentieth century. Businesses the world over – small, medium, large and gargantuan – realised they needed a presence on eBay to maintain a hold on their market.

The effect on the antiques and collectables trade was catastrophic and most of the price catalogues had to be revised. In general terms the effect was to polarise prices. Things that were rare and expensive rose in price, and things that had been collectable but affordable, became more so.

For the first time collectors could reach out to others and cut out the middleman / woman, which spelled disaster for many dealers. In the main, those who shunned the site floundered, whilst those who adapted their trade and embraced it, flourished.

Name the Founder

Most people could name the creator of Facebook but few could put a name to the founder of eBay. Despite radically altering and enhancing the lives of millions of people around the world, the instigator of eBay remains largely unknown. Having made himself and his colleagues into wealthy people, he stepped aside from involvement with the running of eBay to devote himself to philanthropic works. He is an unusual individual who combined a traditional method of selling with cutting-edge technology.

Come in Computers

The story began in the 1950s with the introduction of computers, though it was not until the 1960s that the idea of linking them was first aired. Within a few years this was successfully achieved but initially used solely for military purposes. However, as the final decade of the millennium progressed there were increasing calls for the internet to be made available for commercial use.

Entrepreneurs the world over began to get excited about the possibilities – and they could smell the money. Everyone realised the internet offered sensational opportunities for wealth creation but the big question was 'how'? There followed a frantic gold rush of internet entrepreneurs who threw money at even half credible ideas. Some succeeded but most failed.

Pierre Omidyar

In early 1995 a young man sat down at his computer to write a program. He wanted to create the perfect auction. As it happened he had never attended an auction in his life but understood how they worked and why they attracted buyers. This young man was Pierre Omidyar. So, who is he?

He was born in Paris in 1967 to Iranian parents. His father, a doctor, and his mother, a linguist, had been sent to France by their families to secure them a better education than was then available in Iran.

The lives of the Omidyar family were totally transformed in 1973 when they moved to Baltimore USA, after Pierre's father accepted a residency at John Hopkins University. Unfortunately, they separated soon after the transatlantic move but continued as attentive parents to their only child. Pierre grew up in the USA in the 1970s during the explosion of technology. Like many youngsters, he was fascinated by gadgets, though he soon turned his attention to computers. This interest became an obsession and it soon became clear that he had an aptitude that gave him a label – he was a computer geek.

The first computer he used was a Radio Shack TRS-80 which belonged to his school. Bear in mind this was long before people owned their own PCs. Pierre, the geek, became so keen on it that he missed games to play around on it and soon taught himself to program it using BASIC. It is felt that he inherited linguistic talents from his mother that aided his mastery of the language of computers.

His talents were put to good use and whilst at school he earned pocket money creating useful programs. One was for his school library to computerise their cataloguing and the other was to simplify the timetabling. But, if you are thinking in terms of a model student you would be wrong. Pierre was the first to admit he was not a swot and found it hard to get motivated to complete his school work and mostly only achieved mediocre grades.

Tufts University

However, to his and his parents' relief, he managed to achieve the grades to get him into Tufts University where he studied computer technology. Tufts was a cosmopolitan establishment with an inclusive ethos – a spirit he admired and espoused.

He enjoyed college but remained a mediocre student. However, his expanding skills made it easy for him to gain employment in the college holidays as an intern in Silicon Valley, California. In fact he completed his degree in California where he eventually graduated from the University of California, Berkeley.

It was no great surprise that he chose not to continue his studies but enter the world of work and to take up one of his many offers of employment. During the next few years he gained invaluable experience in various situations, both employed and self-employed, but when an opportunity arose for him to work with the internet for a company called General Magic, he jumped at the chance.

AuctionWeb

However, he was not just a computer geek, he was a creative one and whilst working on his job in the day he would return home to work on his internet idea. He had in mind a global auction that could be accessed by everyone through the power of the internet. He called his auction site AuctionWeb.

AuctionWeb was launched on Labor Day 1995 to a fanfare of indifference – no one looked. However, gradually collectors rolled up, liked what they saw, and informed their friends. It became the talk of the chat rooms and was causing a stir. At this time it was free to users which partly explains why it grew at a such startling rate. AuctionWeb was a huge success – but there was problem.

The service provider was concerned because AuctionWeb was attracting so much traffic that it was slowing down the service. They informed Pierre that they were going to have to levy a charge of $250 a month. Clearly, Pierre did not want to subsidise this from his own pocket on an ongoing basis and he realised that he was going to have to charge his users. But would they be willing to stump up? Bear in mind at this time there was no collection service so he would have to ask them to send the money!

Fee Not Free

The original charges were: 5% of the sale price for items up to $25 and 2.5% of sale price for those over $25.

Pierre feared his users would desert him - but he could not have been more mistaken. Money poured in.

Prolific Growth

AuctionWeb was continually growing and proving profitable which is all the more astonishing at a time when most start-up internet businesses were falling by the wayside.

It was time for Pierre to devote his time to running the site. His first task being to persuade a couple of his colleagues to join him. But there was another problem fast looming.

Most of the transactions went ahead easily and smoothly but when something went wrong traders would email him and expect him to sort it out. Pierre realised that, as membership grew, this would become unmanageable. However, adversity fosters creativity and so this problem provided the inspiration for Feedback, one of the major self-policing tools adopted by websites the world over.

Feedback & Bulletin Board

Feedback is a system by which each trader reports back on the transaction and the conduct of their counterpart. The cumulative comments comprise their reputation by which other members can decide whether or not to deal with them. It has proved enormously successful and the determination to gain positive feedback is one of the central forces in eBay that underlies every transaction. The other innovation was the Bulletin Board whereby perplexed eBay traders looked to others for help.

AuctionWeb renamed eBay

It was at this time that the site, which originally belonged to the Echo Bay Technology Group, was re-branded. Pierre attempted to register the domain name echobay.com but found it was taken by a gold mining company – so shortened it to eBay.com. Pierre realised he had to take his online phenomena to the next level – this required money and expertise.

Benchmark Capital

Pierre knew of a group of internet entrepreneurs known as Benchmark Capital and persuaded a couple of them to attend a meeting. His own enthusiasm was such that, with no business plan, he believed the site would speak for itself.

Sadly, at the time of the meeting, in the days when the internet was unreliable, they were unable to access the site and the Benchmark representatives left the room totally underwhelmed. However, on arriving home, one of them, Bob Kagle, decided to take a look at eBay and instantly realised it would hit the spot with collectors. Won over, he persuaded his colleagues and the required funding, $6.5 million, was made available.

Talent at the Top

Next came the search for an inspirational leader. This was not an easy task as the internet was still in its infancy and experienced executives were thin on the ground. However, they approached and headhunted Meg Whitworth, who had a track record of success with an array of companies. It was at this time that Pierre Omidyar stepped aside to concentrate on his philanthropic works. Under new leadership eBay continued to grow and the site that started with no visitors has a turnover that is now expressed in billions of dollars. It is infused into modern culture and widely regarded as 'the peoples' site'.

eBay UK

eBay UK was launched in 1999. It is estimated that over 19 million Britons visit eBay every month and over 200,000 people in this country earn some or all of their income through eBay.

Landmark Development Timeline

1967	Pierre Omidyar born in Paris, France
1984	Attends Tufts University
1988	Graduates from University of California, Berkeley
1988	Works at Innovative Data Design & Claris
1991	Co-founds Ink Development Corporation
1994	Joins General Magic to work with internet
1995	Creates AuctionWeb
1996	Gives up day job to become CEO
1997	AuctionWeb renamed eBay
1997	Benchmark Capital invests $6.5 million in eBay
1998	Meg Whitman headhunted as CEO of eBay
	eBay offers stock shares to the public
	Omidyar Network launched

1999	eBay UK launched
2001	Profits for eBay rise $24.6 million in 3 months
2002	PayPal purchased (sold in 2015)
2005	Skype purchased (sold in 2011)
2014	eBay total revenue $17.9 billion
2014	eBay mobile payment volume $45.6 billion

eBay Overview

Trading Options

In the beginning eBay was purely an auction site. However, its rapid and remarkable growth inevitably lead to its diversification into other modes of trading. The options are:

Auction

An online auction that lasts for a specified time (up to 10 days) whereby the highest bidder wins the item.

Buy It Now

An item is offered for a specified time at a set price. The auction is concluded when a buyer makes the purchase. Sellers can also list multiple identical items for individual purchase.

Auction with Buy It Now

A timed auction with a Buy It Now price (BIN) for anyone wishing to avoid the wait and buy instantly. The BIN price is higher than the start price but, as soon as a bid is placed, the BIN disappears and it becomes a regular auction.

Buy It Now or Best Offer

An item is listed with a stated price but the seller will consider offers. When an offer is submitted the seller can decline or accept (or make a counter offer.) If the seller accepts the offer, the transaction is binding

to both parties. (If the counter offer is accepted by the buyer, the transaction is also binding.)

eBay Shops

Online shops with a stock of items that are offered at a set price.

eBay – the Basics

- eBay brings together buyers and sellers

- There are a variety of trading options

- eBay do not usually become involved in the transaction

- Buyers pay sellers direct

- The money should be secured before the goods are sent

- Items go direct from seller to buyer

- Items are not vetted by eBay

- Traders must be over 18 years old

- You have to register to trade on eBay

- It's free to buy but sellers pay a fee

- eBay is a community where members police the site

- PayPal is eBay's preferred payment system

- PayPal is free to buyers but sellers pay a fee

- Click & Collect is increasingly offered by sellers

- Many sellers offer a returns policy (usually 14 days)

Understanding the Features

To flourish on eBay you need to understand the key concepts and features that oil the works of the site.

Feedback

This is your reputation on the site and is vital to your success as a trader. You only need to glance at a trader's feedback score to get an idea of their reliability. Fortunately feedback also works as a deterrent to poor practice, as most eBay traders work hard to avoid negative feedback. It's so important to get this right that an entire chapter is devoted to feedback.

cherrypiex (768 ⭐)

100% Positive Feedback

Global Postage

An innovation whereby sellers can open their auctions up to international buyers on the basis that they send the sold item to a UK depot from where it will be forwarded. The international postage and customs paperwork, where it applies, is completed for the seller and it is also tracked from the UK shipping centre. The advantage to the seller is that the item is likely to sell for a higher price. (The potential downside is when the item is unsatisfactory and needs to be returned.) Not all items qualify for this scheme.

Returns

Some buyers have concerns about purchasing an item that they cannot handle and examine. In order to address this worry sellers can decide to offer a returns policy. A buyer must return the item, usually at their own expense, within 14 days and in the same condition as they received it. It undoubtedly promotes trust and indicates the seller's confidence in their goods.

What Can You Buy?

Just about anything. Shoes, clothes and accessories for women and men, both new and used. Televisions, laptops, mobile phones and tablets sell like hot cakes.

There is everything for the home on eBay including second-hand kitchen units and fencing panels etc. Interior designers use eBay as a sourcing tool. They can browse a particular category such as Art Deco or state the colour in the keyword search.

Mundane everyday items - stationary, floss - can be found on eBay and often at discount prices. They can be delivered to your home so that you save on the cost of petrol and parking.

Collectables thrive on eBay which enables enthusiasts to fill the gap in their collections from the comfort of their homes and make like-minded friends. eBay negates mobility issues for collectors.

Short breaks, holidays, courses and services can be found at a fraction of the regular price – but do your research.

What Sells Best

Buyers love clothes with labels and branded goods. It probably comes as no surprise that designer labels excite the shoppers but all labels, including M&S, Topshop and Next, are a bonus as they give the buyer an idea of the calibre of the garment.

Branded goods fare well as they define the quality. Unwanted or duplicate gifts, particularly when boxed and in pristine condition, fetch good prices. Otherwise be clear about condition.

The antiques trade thrives on eBay and items from specific eras - Victorian, Twenties, Fifties - are snapped up.

New mums make a beeline for eBay. Baby related items are often used for a short time and can be passed on at fair prices.

Top Tips for Savvy Traders

- Bargain hunters should look out for auctions that are ending soon and seek out those with no bids.

- Buyers should pay with PayPal. It's quick, convenient, free, includes safeguards and saves the cost of a stamp.

- eBay auctions attract lower prices in the summer, so do your Christmas shopping on eBay in August.

- Select auctions with free P&P.

- To avoid getting landed with something unsuitable, seek out sellers who accept returns. You will probably have to pay return postage but at least you will not be stuck with it.

- Buy your DVDs on eBay so that you can watch them at your leisure before selling them on.

- Buy special occasion outfits on eBay, taking care to note the condition and checking out the seller. Sensational wedding hats sell for a fraction of high street prices - no one need know!

- Entrepreneurial sellers should look out for popular collectable items to sell. Many items that originate in the UK have a strong global appeal, which is reflected in the price.

What's lurking in your loft? This Dr Who Annual 1969 stunned the owner when it fetch £115 in a recent eBay auction. It underlies the power of eBay and the global market.

Understanding eBay Buying

- Undertake a search to find an item

- Browse the categories and sub-categories

- Or undertake and refine a keyword search

- Study the information on the auction page

- Scrutinise the pictures

- New or used - what condition?

- Discover the cost of shipping

- Can you comply with the method of payment?

- Check the feedback of the seller

- If concerned read feedback comments

- Contact the seller via link with questions

- If still keen, place a bid

- Watch the auction progress in My eBay

- If outbid - bid again or look elsewhere

- On winning the item use link in My eBay to pay

- Check the item as soon as it arrives

- All well? If so, leave positive feedback

- Receive positive feedback from seller

Understanding eBay Selling

- Put an item up for auction

- Add multiple pictures

- List the item in an appropriate category

- Use all possible keywords in the auction title

- Describe the item including flaws

- State the length of the auction

- Carefully choose the start price

- Or accept eBay's suggested start price

- Research and state the cost of shipping

- Or accept eBay's suggested P&P

- Consider using a reserve price (£50+)

- Watch the auction and answer questions

- The winner receives an email from eBay

- The seller can send an online invoice via links

- Or the buyer pays (includes P & P) via the links

- Carefully packs and sends the item

- The delighted buyer leaves positive feedback

- Leave positive feedback for your buyer

eBay UK Home Page

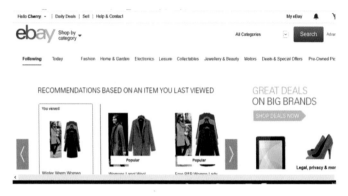

Type 'eBay UK' into your search engine to come up with links to the site which you will enter via the homepage. It has a vibrant and busy homepage that, on first sight, looks daunting. However it largely consists of links to instigate various tasks the most important of which, for novices, are:

Categories and eBay Search Engine

Just beneath the links you will find Categories beside the Search box. These are the links that offer the various alternatives for finding what you want. You can opt for the slower, more leisurely pace of shopping on eBay by browsing the categories and sub-categories.

Keywords

Alternatively, you can go direct to what you want by typing in the keywords and clicking enter. The resulting list of auctions can be refined to speed up your search. If the results reveal auctions that are not of interest you need to think again about the keywords you have used.

Homepage Links

At the top of the homepage on the left-hand side are links marked Daily Deals, Sell and Help & Contact and on the right-hand side is the link to My eBay and the shopping basket.
Daily Deals lure you towards the current special offers.

Daily Deals | Sell | Help & Contact

Sell Link

Sell is the link that enables you to start the process of creating an auction – though you need to master buying before you try.

Help & Contact

Help & Contact offers a wide range of options for assistance. Rest the cursor on the link to reveal your options.

My eBay

My eBay is where you will find everything relating to your eBay activities including your bidding, buying and selling. You will access My eBay every time you log on. It is the start point from which you will instigate your follow up activities, using the links provided. It is where you will find your account information and incorporates measures for keeping you safe. In fact, My eBay is so important an entire chapter is devoted to it.

The basket provides an opportunity to pay for several separate purchases with one transaction. The bell symbol alerts you to outstanding notifications, which might include reminders that an auction you are watching is coming to an end and messages from other traders. Click on it when there is a number beside it to view the most recent notifications.

Other Useful Links

At the very bottom of most pages (not the homepage) is a list of significant links which, despite their low key position, are extremely useful. They include: About eBay, Announcements, Community, Safety Centre, Help & Contact and Site Map.

About eBay   Announcements   Community   Safety Centre

Help & Contact   Site Map

About eBay and Announcements - give the latest information on the site, developments and changes.

Community - this aspect of eBay has always been central. Members support each other with help and advice and there are numerous opportunities to confer and commiserate in the various chat forums. There are a vast number of discussion groups and online clubs. Whatever your interest you are bound to find like minds in eBay's community. Autograph hunting thrives on eBay and the collectors share their enthusiasm. (This signed picture of Sir Bruce Forsyth sold for £30.)

Safety Centre and Resolution Centre - have evolved from years of experience of sorting out the trading problems that occur from time to time. eBay prefer members to settle differences between themselves but if this fails, they will intervene.

Site Map

Site Map is an extremely useful link that consists a summary of everything that eBay contains and offers clarity. If you have a problem that requires specific action you will likely find a link to the way forward in Site Map.

Feedback

Your Online Reputation

To understand feedback you need to consider the importance of a reputation. In seeking a plumber you would seek one who is highly rated by previous clients and actively avoid someone with a poor track record. Feedback is the online equivalent of a reputation, but one that is detailed and totally accessible.

Originally, identical feedback opportunities were available to both buyer and seller. More recently, feedback was adapted in favour of buyers to ensure that they were free to report openly about the trade, without fear of negative feedback retaliation. Sellers are invited to leave feedback but the options are limited to positive or neutral - though, if they feel justified and inclined, they can post a seething comment.

How Feedback Works

On receiving the goods, and providing everyone is happy, the buyer completes a brief affirmative report on the seller. There may be rare occasions when a buyer has a bad experience which needs to be conveyed to the community. The comments, collectively referred to as feedback, are helpful to other traders.

Feedback Form

There are three aspects to the feedback form:

1.   Rating – Positive, Negative or Neutral

2.   Statement – how it went (examples above)

3.   Detailed Seller Rating – completed by buyers only

Feedback Rating – Score

Beside each User ID is the trader's score which is part of the unfolding story of their feedback. The feedback rating can be positive, neutral or negative. Positive awards a point, neutral has no value and negative loses a point. A trader's feedback score is the difference between the number of positive and negative ratings. (It is slightly different for multiple sales and depends if the sales occurred in different weeks.)

Feedback Rating – Percentage

Feedback is also expressed as a percentage which offers a useful overview of different traders' abilities to resolve disputes, levelling the playing field by evaluating exchanges out of 100.

Score and Percentage in Combination

When used together it's extremely helpful as just a glance at the score and percentage offers an insight into the likely reliability of a trader. However, sometimes negative feedback is left unfairly and you have an opportunity to read the comment, (and response by the seller to them) to decide about the trader for yourself. To do this click on to **See detailed feedback.**

Check the seller's reputation
Score: 225 | 94.1% Positive
See detailed feedback

This seller has only achieved 94.1% positive feedback on 255 transactions. You should read the feedback comments before trading with this eBayer.

No such concerns about this trader's track record of 100% positive on over 19,000 transactions!

Check the seller's reputation
Score: 19575 | 100% Positive
See detailed feedback

Feedback Time Chart – Recent or Historic

You can also opt to view a seller's feedback mapped out on a time chart. Historic negative feedback is not considered to be as concerning as more recent failings. Also you need to consider the number of negative ratings set against the total number of trades in that period. Two poor ratings are significant in the past month if they are the only two trades.

		1 month	6 months	12 months
⊕	Positive	59	367	693
◉	Neutral	0	1	3
⊖	Negative	2	2	2

Where To Leave Feedback

The links are in different sections of My eBay:

Buyers - My eBay - Purchase History - Feedback link on right

Sellers - My eBay - Sold - Feedback link on right

Feedback Form – Buyer to Complete

The form (for the buyer) leads you through the process. First, and most critical, is the part that affects their reputation at a glance. You rate the trade a positive, neutral or negative. This is usually positive - never leave a negative rating without giving the seller an opportunity to correct the shortfalls or make amends. For this part the seller has a similar form but without the opportunity to leave a negative rating.

Rate this transaction

◉ Positive   ○ Neutral   ○ Negative   ○ I'll leave Feedback later

Feedback Statement

Feedback allows both buyer and seller to say a few words about the transaction and traders usually enter into this wholeheartedly. eBay encourage constructive comments that explain the praise.

Tell us more

I absolutely love this skirt. Great service too. Thanks so much.

15 characters left

Cumulative Comments

Comments can be found with the trader's feedback score and give an idea of what you can expect from them.

⊕ Immediate dispatch, arrived within 24 hours, lovely item

Star By Julien Macdonald Purple Satin Feel Tailored Sexy F (#181993709711)

⊕ Speedy delivery. Looks great, fits well. So pleased. Thankyc

Detailed Seller Rating

This section is for buyers only and invites detailed star ratings on different aspects of the trade. It's quick and anonymous and helps to keep sellers on their toes. More recently it asks if the seller achieved the estimated delivery time.

Item as described	★★★★⯪
Communication	★★★★⯪
Dispatch time	★★★★⯪
Postage and packaging charges	★★★★⯪

Did the item arrive on or before Wednesday, 03 February 2016?

● Yes ○ No

Must I leave Feedback?

Would you leave a shop without saying thank you to an assistant who had provided good service? Feedback is the online equivalent of saying thank you and is at the heart of eBay's community ethos.

Steve was delighted with the Victorian tobacco box he bought to add to his collection. He enjoyed excellent service from the seller which was reflected in his effusive feedback. The seller posted constructive praise that highlighted the speedy payment.

Leaving Negative Feedback

What about negative feedback? Should I never leave negative feedback? If no one was prepared to leave negative feedback the concept would be worthless. However, leaving negative feedback is a very last resort and should only be left when everything else has failed. If a seller makes a mistake, but tries everything reasonable to make amends, you should leave positive feedback. However, the eBay community need to be warned about fraudulent traders.

Seller Feedback

Poor practice is not just confined to rogue sellers. Sometimes buyers fall short of the mark with slow payment and unreasonable demands. Frustrated sellers are no longer able to warn others about a tiresome buyer by leaving negative feedback but can leave positive feedback taking the opportunity to reveal their shortcomings in a measured statement.

How to Secure Positive Feedback

As a Buyer

- Study the pictures with care
- Make no assumptions about the item
- Ask seller a question and assess their tone
- Pay quickly
- Check the item as soon as it arrives
- Get straight back to the seller with concerns
- Ensure all communications are courteous

As a Seller

- Describe with care
- Provide plenty of pictures from all angles
- Include dimensions and scale
- Offer a returns option
- Be clear about delivery times
- Send item promptly
- Be attentive to your buyer throughout the process
- Listen sympathetically to your buyer's concerns

The seller of this fine vintage radio described it with enormous care, treading a delicate path between accuracy and enthusiasm. His efforts paid dividends when he received glowing feedback from his buyer

Payment

Paying for an Item

At some point, successful transactions involve an exchange of funds. From online-type payment methods to the handing over of cash, there are numerous means of paying for items and the optimum method often depends on the nature of the item.

However, the bottom line is that all sellers are required to offer PayPal as one of the payment options. Buyers who seek alternatives need to check, before bidding on items, that they are able to comply with the sellers' payment requirements. Methods of payments accepted are found on the auction page.

eBay Permitted Payment

- PayPal

- Credit cards

- Bank transfers

- Online payment services - various

- Cheques

- Postal orders

- Payment on collection

Sellers – How to Select Payment Options

Sellers state how they accept payment when they create their auction. You can tailor your requirements to suit each item though in many ways the more options you offer, the better. It's your choice and entirely flexible.

Payment methods accepted

PayPal ℹ

PayPal email address ℹ

Make sure your PayPal email a

☐ Personal cheque

☐ Postal order

Buyers - How to Find Payment Options

Payments:

PayPal [MasterCard] **VISA** [Maestro] [_____] Processed by PayPal ,
Postal order/Banker's draft | See payment information

As you can see from the previous page there are many alternatives for payment but, as a buyer, you have to make sure you can comply. It is important that buyers check this before they place a bid. However, the bottom line is that you will always be able to pay using PayPal. If you don't want to pay this way you must ensure there is another suitable option. You will find this information at the top-centre of the auction page, beneath the box to place your bid.

My eBay - Purchase History

Select a payment option

PayPal

Credit or debit card ℹ

On winning an item you need to progress the purchase in My eBay - Purchase History. Locate the item and click on the title to access the auction, where you will discover the methods of payment offered by the seller. Select whichever method suits you best.

PayPal on eBay

When eBay started out there was a problem over payment of goods bought overseas and some traders resorted to sending dollars in the post! Fortunately this has been resolved by PayPal, which has made payment easy as well as offering protection. Buyers should open up a PayPal account for their eBay trading however, you can use it for payment of a wide variety of goods and services. Furthermore it's free for buyers.

PayPal Sold Off

In 2002 eBay bought PayPal and it was seamlessly integrated into the site enabling traders to access their PayPal accounts and use it to pay their fees. Although PayPal is no longer owned by eBay the close association continues and traders can still access their PayPal account via My eBay. However, one resulting change is that communications from PayPal are no longer displayed in My eBay - Messages.

My Account
- Personal information
- Addresses
- Communication preferences
- Site preferences
- Manage communications with buyers
- Seller Dashboard
- Feedback
- PayPal account
- Seller account
- Donation account

Is PayPal Secure?

The security of PayPal is the number one concern. Are you really going to give out such sensitive financial details? PayPal employs encryption technology to protect your financial details. Using PayPal means you avoid sending a complete stranger a cheque with your bank details and sample of your signature!

PayPal Fees

For Buyers - to make a payment is free

For Sellers - to receive funds costs 3.4% + 20p

(Slightly more for cross-border payments)

Advantages of PayPal for Buyers

- PayPal is free to buyers

- Payment arrives instantly

- There are no cheques to clear

- The goods arrive sooner

- PayPal offers buyer protection

- Mobility issues and cost of getting to bank do not apply

Advantages of PayPal for Sellers

- The convenience of PayPal attracts buyers

- PayPal offers seller protection

- PayPal facilitates global transactions

- The money arrives instantly

Requirements for a PayPal Account

- Email address

- Postal address

- Phone number

- Credit card or debit card

- Bank account details

Creating a PayPal Account

There are two different kinds of account:

- Personal Account - non-professional traders
- Business Account - professional traders

Overview of Setting Up a PayPal Account

- Go to PayPal website – www.paypal.co.uk
- Select 'Sign Up' to create PayPal account
- Complete the form
- Think of a password
- Receive PayPal email and confirm password
- Enter debit and/or credit card details
- Enter bank account details
- Receive PayPal email and follow 'confirm' instructions to lift withdrawal limits on your PayPal account.

You don't need money in your PayPal account to buy something. Linking your bank account details or any credit/debit card to your PayPal account allows you to start trading.

Alternatively, if you'd like to add funds to your PayPal account you can do this yourself from a linked account or let PayPal do it for you if you complete the Direct Debit instruction via PayPal.

Verify Who You Are

PayPal initially sets a limit on the amount you can receive into your PayPal account to £1,700 per annum. If your PayPal account is likely to receive more than this amount you can remove the limit by going through an extra step that confirms that you are who you say you are. It is important to do this:

- To give other traders complete confidence in you
- To remove financial limitations on your trading
- To offer full PayPal benefits

How to Verify Who You Are

- Go to your PayPal account at www.paypal.co.uk
- Click 'View Your Account Limits' from the bottom of the Summary page
- Click 'Confirm Your Personal Information' on next page
- You will be guided through the process for verification

Verification Process Involves

- Confirming your identity
- Complying with EU law
- Enhancing your trading status

PayPal Summary Page

The Summary page offers an overview of your account including account balance, linked credit/debit cards and/or bank account as well as links to tools, further information and account activity. You can hold funds in several different currencies or, if you prefer, you can change them to pounds sterling.

PayPal Link

P PayPal | Summary | **Activity** | **Send and Request** | **Wallet**

The Summary page offers links to allow you to undertake various activities and make the most of and move around your account. These links include:

- Activity – Overview of all fund transactions
- Send And Request – Send money or Request payment
- Wallet – Details of linked funding sources

Paying Via PayPal

To pay for an item you have bought on eBay with PayPal you simply select this as the payment method.

Total: £3.79 GBP

○ PayPal account (login required)

Receiving Funds Via PayPal

If you receive a payment through PayPal you will receive an email notification that the funds are in your PayPal account.

PayPal

Hello C E Hixon,

You received a payment of

Your Profile

The Summary page also contains the Settings icon at the top right-hand corner. Click on this to change any of your personal details, security details or notification preferences.

Account History

Payment received	+ £29.50	– £1.20	+ £28.30
Purchase	– £4.18	£0.00	– £4.18

The Activity page of your PayPal account itemises every transaction that you have undertaken. PayPal do not charge buyers for sending payment but sellers are charged a fee. However, PayPal clearly show the fees charged, which is the difference between the Gross Amount and the Net Amount. For buyers the gross sum and net sum are the same.

Adding/Withdrawing Funds

Use the Wallet link to update details of your credit/debit cards and/or bank accounts. Using the Wallet link you can move funds between your bank and PayPal accounts - funds are transferred within hours.

Examples of PayPal Fees

Sold – Leather Satchel Shoulder Bag

High Bid: £5.10
Postage: £2.80
Funds sent: £7.90
Payment received: £7.43
PayPal Fee: £0.47

Sold – Boxed Dinky Fire Engine 1952

High bid: £26.00
Postage: £3.50
Funds sent: £29.50
Payment Received: £28.30
PayPal Fee: £1.20

Sold – An Huang Solid Silicone Baby Doll

High bid: £3,650.00
Postage: Free
Funds sent: £3,650.00
Payment received: £3,525.70
PayPal Fee: £124.30

Sold – Vintage Leather Women's Shoes

High Bid: £10.72
Postage: £3.50
Funds sent: £14.22
Payment received: £13.54
PayPal Fee: £0.68

Get Organised

Suggested Strategy for Success

Starting out on eBay is rather like learning to drive. We would be horrified for non-drivers to get behind the wheel and kangaroo off into the traffic without instruction. It takes time and commitment. eBay trading also presents a learning curve in which you need to familiarise yourself with the processes, rules and conventions. Start out cautiously and methodically and build up your feedback score.

How to Proceed:

- For your first 20 transactions focus on your feedback. Positive feedback is critical. Ideally all your feedback should be positive but for your first transactions it's vital.

- Always start with buying. It's easier than selling and will introduce you to the process and the concerns of buyers.

- Your first transactions should be unambitious. Purchase an everyday item from a UK trader.

- When selling for the first time make sure it's something straightforward and simple.

- Offer your buyers a returns option.

- Make your auctions sound courteous and friendly. Welcome all questions and spell out a desire to please.

Get Organised for the Long Term

Whether you intend to use eBay occasionally or regularly you should set yourself up for long term trading. You need to:

Set Up Finances

You should consider opening up a new bank account for your eBay activities. This allows you to keep your eBay finances separate from your other financial incomings and outgoings. You might consider going a security step further by opening up a new bank account in an alternative bank. Whatever you decide, link your PayPal account to this bank account. Your eBay finances will be separate and easy to track.

Set Up As a Buyer

- Choose a User Name
- Choose a password
- Register as an eBay buyer
- Open up a PayPal Account

Set Up As a Seller

- Create eBay Picture Folders
- Arrange your finances
- Register as a seller when creating your first sale
- Choose to pay eBay selling fees with PayPal

Choose a Unique User Name

This is the name by which you are known to other traders and needs to be unique. eBay understand the potential difficulty in coming up with a unique username and suggest one you might like to use, or recommend similar alternatives if you choose a name that has already been taken. Whatever you decide, make it something that you can easily recall.

Choose a Password

In choosing your password you need to think up something that you can remember but which no-one else would guess.

Step by Step Register to Buy

- Enter your email address and password
- Enter your name
- Enter your mobile phone number
- Read and accept eBay User Agreement and consent to the processing of your data

Click Register

View the screen acknowledgement – Welcome to eBay, Cherry!

Create User Name

Create unique user name by either:

Accepting eBay's suggestion

Composing your own

Welcome to eBay, Cherry!

We've created a unique username for you: **chernixo0**

Continue

OR

Customise your username

Click **Confirm** to go to eBay homepage to start your search

Buy Your First Item

You will be requested to provide further information to facilitate your first transaction, which should be buying. To complete this trade you need to provide your address.

Click on **Continue**

First Purchase Payment

Select PayPal as a payment option

Log in to PayPal by entering your password

Confirm & Pay

Thanks your order was placed!

ebay Checkout

Select a payment option

PayPal

Credit or debit card

Register as a Seller

Register as a seller whilst creating your first auction. It's easy to follow the steps that start with clicking on the **Sell** link.

ebay

Tell us what you're selling

Work your way through the auction creation form – described in Chapter 11. When you have completed the details click on the link to list your item. You are diverted to a new screen where you are lead through the steps to complete registration.

Take the link to sign in again to make changes to your account and confirm your contact information

- Confirm or edit your address
- Confirm your mobile phone number
- Receive PIN on your mobile phone
- Choose between – **Call me now** or **Text me now**

Enter the PIN where indicated on your screen.

Select Payment Type – Choose from:
- PayPal
- Credit / Credit Card
- Bank Account

(PayPal is recommended for ease of set-up because your financial details held by PayPal can be used in this process.)

Continue to PayPal and log in to set up preapproved payments to automatically pay your eBay seller fees. Note this is flexible – you can change this arrangement at any time.

Confirm or edit your Payment Details
Click link to agree.
Congratulations your item is now listed for sale.

Selling – Create Picture Folders

It pays dividends to get organised from the outset. You need to create the following folders:

- eBay Selling
- eBay Sold

eBay Selling

Shoulder Bag
Front

Shoulder bag
side

Snoopy 2

Soweby Pressed
Glass

Spice tin open

Spice tin

Spoon tray 1780

Tea Caddy 1820

Victorian Mirror -

Vinaigrette open

Digital photography and phone cameras take on a whole new significance when it comes to eBay. It enables you to take lots of photographs, upload them into your eBay Selling folder and then delete all but the best. Do not keep duplicates, just those that you intend to use in your auctions, and change the file name of each picture to identify it. Your eBay SELL file is an uncluttered working file for pictures to use in your auctions.

eBay Sold

When you have sold an item transfer it to **eBay Sold** and change the file name to the price achieved. In time this will provide you with a useful archive of eBay prices. Depending on how prolific you become as a seller, you may want to open a new **eBay Sold** file each year.

£18.05

£18.30

£24.00

£55

£78.00

4.59

Download the eBay App

The App offers a quantum leap in convenience. It's quick to master, easy to use and installing it is simple. Depending on exactly what operating system your device uses you need to go to Google Play or the App Store and tap on the links.

Android

The most popular operating system is Android and if your tablet or smart phone is based on Android (Samsung, HTC, Google, Sony, LG etc) you should go to the Google Play icon to find the eBay App. You may need to set up a Google Account which is easy to do just follow the links.

Apple

The next is Apple so if you use an Apple iPad or iPhone you need to locate the eBay App in the App Store on your device.

Blackberry & Windows

The other operating systems are for Blackberry smart phones, tablets or Windows based devices. Although an eBay App is available for both Blackberry devices and Windows based tablets and smart phones the eBay App for these devices are outdated. The screen images throughout this section are from the latest version of the eBay App which is, currently, only available on Android or Apple devices.

To Install

• Go to Google Play or App Store and tap the search link.

• Type in eBay App to bring up the list

• Tap on the eBay App (at top of the list) to select it

• Select install and accept terms and conditions

My eBay

Finding My eBay

My eBay: Summary   cherrypiex (769★)

Activity   Messages   Account

You will find the link to My eBay at the top of the home page. You need to familiarise yourself with My eBay as it's your unique space that is central to most of your activities. You should think of My eBay as your house in that everything in it concerns you and only you can go there. You will probably go to My eBay every time you visit the site. More importantly much of your activity will commence from the links you find there and it plays a major role in keeping you safe from fraud.

My eBay is divided into four sections but only three of these need concern new comers.

- Activity

- Messages

- Account

Click on the tag to take you to the appropriate section.

Summary of Activities

On the left-hand side of My eBay you will find the summary of your activities. These consist of your purchase history, your watch lists, the searches you follow, the sellers you follow and all of your selling activity. The most critical are the summaries of your buying and selling. It's important that you progress these activities via the links in My eBay.

Sell

The sell link is particularly important. The example shown of the left hand side indicate that there are three active or ongoing auctions.

One is marked as scheduled, which means that the seller has created an auction but has delayed the start. This auction will begin at a time chosen by the seller.

The example shows four saved drafts. The process of creating an auction is so flexible that you can retain information and pictures in draft to complete and activate later.

Sell

All selling

Sell an item

Saved drafts (4)

Scheduled (1)

Active (3)

Sold (1)

Unsold (1)

Active

Click on the Active link to view your auctions. They are listed with a reminder of the main features – title and picture. To view the auction page click on the auction title.

Ladies Real Leath
& F - Used (20145
High bidder: joh
(514 ⭐)

New Hall Tea Bow
Porcelain (201459

Active also shows how many people are watching your auctions It shows the number of bids and current price (those with bids in green). It states the time left.

Sold

When you sell an item you will come to My eBay and click on the sold link to access the completed auction. This will provide you will the information and links to progress the sale.

Watch

You can follow an auction without placing a bid by putting it into your watch list. There are several reasons that you might want to do this including to enable you to do your research. Many buyers like to place a bid towards the end of the auction. You will find a link at the top right hand side of the auction page (underneath the item number). Click the link to place it in your watch list.

Buy

At the top of the page is the summary of all buying activity. If you have placed a bid on an item you will find it in Active. Click on this link to see how the auction is progressing and to check on the current price and the number of bids. If you bid on an item but fail to win it, you can check on the final price in Didn't Win!

Reminders

My eBay also offers reminders of your outstanding tasks. The icons shown above light up when they are completed. The activity section of My eBay also offers convenient links to progress these tasks (as shown above) and help you to gain positive feedback.

Searches & Sellers You Follow

All kinds of motivated buyers find this feature handy. You can save searches for keywords or categories, which means that eBay send you an email to inform you of these auctions. Click on the link to reveal a summary of your saved searches .

How to Save a Search

When you undertake a keyword search the number of results are shown at the top of the page before the list of auctions. To the right of this is a link to save the search. Click on the link to save the search and increase the number of saved searches.

▾ Lists

All lists
Watch list
Wish list
Your lists

Searches you follow

How to Save a Seller

You will find the **Add to Favourite Sellers** link in the top right hand section of the auction page in Meet the Seller.

 | Add to Watch list

Sheila is a keen collector of Crested China. Trading on eBay has enabled her to fill many of the gaps in her collection. She has no concerns about missing anything as she has saved keywords searches, as well as sellers who deal in these pieces, to ensure she is notified each time something of interest to her comes up for auction.

Messages

Activity   Messages (6)   Account

eBay work constantly to improve the site and keep it safe. An important innovation was the introduction of Messages which has arisen because of the concern about fraudulent emails. Such emails are attempts by cheats to get hold of the IDs and passwords of unsuspecting eBay

All messages (6)

From members (2)

From eBay (4)

! High priority

traders for criminal purposes. Significant communications are duplicated in Messages. When you receive an email that appears to be from eBay, regarding your account, you should first check to see if it's in Messages. You can access the message by clicking on the title.

What you will find in Messages

- Important alerts from eBay about your account.
- Useful messages from eBay about buying and selling activities and events
- When you ask a seller a question or reply to a question you will find the communications in Messages
- Offers and special deals from eBay

I have a question about using my item or I want to send the selle Ended

Your eBay invoice for November is now ready to view   --

Thanks for selling this year. Accept your 100 free listings reward --

Account

| Activity | Messages | **Account** | Applications 🆕 |

If My eBay equates to your house, Account is the study inside your house. This is the part that contains the administrative and financial aspects of your eBay trading. If you change your address, bank, or replace a credit card, you should click on the link to make appropriate amendments.

Communication Preferences

eBay like to keep their members informed and their default setting is to send you emails to confirm all your activity. However, prolific traders can find themselves bombarded with these messages. eBay give you the opportunity to tailor these notifications. Click on the link to access the notification options.

Feedback

Click on the Feedback link to access all the feedback you have posted, received and all that is outstanding.

PayPal

Until recently, PayPal was owned by eBay and much was done to integrate the sites. You can still access your PayPal account by the 'back door' by using this link. Use your PayPal password to access your account.

My account

Personal information

Addresses

Communication preferences

Site preferences

Manage communications with buyers

Seller Dashboard

Feedback

PayPal account

Seller account

Donation account

Subscriptions

Resolution Centre

Seller Account

This is where you check your accounts. eBay are meticulous about breaking down their charges and making them crystal clear to their users. You can check on the status of your account and change the way you pay the charges.

Finding Things

Buying Starts with Searching

Even if you are primarily interested in selling you need to experience the buying process as it will undoubtedly enable you to create better auctions.

The process begins with finding what you want from the millions of items for sale at any one time. There are two methods of finding things: you can either undertake a keyword search or browse the categories.

Browsing the Categories

Every single item that is offered for sale is placed in a category. This means that buyers can browse through the various sections to find what they want to buy. The Categories link is found on every page on the site including on the Home page.

Keyword Search

Searching for an item involves typing keywords into the search bar (found at the top of the page) and clicking on the Search button. This will reveal a list of auctions that will hopefully be of interest. If not, adapt your keywords and try again.

Category Search

The most leisurely way to shop on eBay is to browse the categories. You will find the link at the top of the homepage and can work your way through the subcategories until you come to the list of auctions. It's possible that there are too many auctions to reasonably consider, in which event you can use the options on the left-hand side of the page to focus your search.

Watches

Wristwatches

Pocket Watches

Fob & Nurse Watches

Ring Watches

Key Ring Watches

Necklace Watches

Wristwatch Straps

Batteries

Parts, Tools & Guides

Target Your Search

When looking for a watch you can narrow it down by selecting the type you require (as shown). You can choose to see a particular make of watch. Lower down the list of options you can also select the condition you require. It is also possible to state the parameters on price so that you see nothing too cheap or too costly. To speed things up you can view the Buy It Now auctions or just consider those with Free P&P.

Clue in the Title

Ensure that you take in every word in the title, including faux, style and type.

- Faux leather - this is not leather or suede but a synthetic material.
- Fifties style - this is a modern copy of the look.
- Clarice Cliff type - a much less valuable copy of the original.

Making the Most of Keyword Search

When embarking on a search, type the keywords connected with the item you seek into the search bar to reveal the list of auctions. For example:

Road Bike Adult

More or Less

If your initial keyword search reveals too many auctions you should put another word into the search engine. This will likely result in a shorter list of more appropriate auctions. If the initial results reveal too few you might consider removing a word to reveal more auctions.

Frame Size

☐ **18"** (2)

☐ **19.5"** (1)

☐ **26"** (20)

☐ **54cm** (4)

This search – Adult Road Bike – (Cycling Category selected) revealed over 1,000 auction results but the options on the left-hand side allow you to pinpoint your search. You can select the brand of bike, the number of gears and size of frame as well as the colour etc.

As with a category search, you can use the standard options on the left-hand side which enable you to choose:

- Category
- New or Used
- Price Level
- Within UK or International
- Auction or Buy It Now

Auction Results Summaries

Look through the auction results until you find a summary and picture that interests you. Click on the title to access the auction page giving all the details about the auction.

Sort By

Once you are happy with the list of auctions the search has revealed you need to sort them in a way that is helpful. The sort function at the top of the page is very useful.

The **sort by** option enables you to easily find the most affordable item, so you can track down the cheapest second hand copy of 'Gone Girl'.

Keyword search 'Gone Girl'
From left hand side select Categories for books.

Then move to the sort by option at the top of the page and select:
'Price: lowest first'.

The list of auctions will come up in price order, the least expensive first. Make sure you carefully examine the auction page and also note the feedback of the seller.

Price: lowest first ▾

Time: ending soonest

Time: newly listed

Price + P&P: lowest first

Price + P&P: highest first

Price: highest first

Distance: nearest first

Condition: new first

Distance: Nearest First

A very useful option is the one that concerns the location of the item. When you are buying items that you intend to collect in person or pay to ship, it is prudent to find something that is not too far away. The distance option re-organises the list showing  the closest first and indicating how far away in miles they are. This information is shown in the auction summary so that you can see at a glance the item's approximate proximity.

Auction Page

Ladies Real Leather Brown Handbag F & F - Used

Condition: **Used**

Ends in: 2h 34m 32s (06 Nov. 2015 13:30:40 GMT)

£7.70 8 bids

Enter your max bid

Submit bid

Add to Watch list ▼   ★ **Add to collection**

Seller information

cherrypiex (765 ★)

100% Positive Feedback

See other Items

Click on the auction title to access the auction page and view the live auction. The auction page conforms to a format:

Top on the left-hand side is a large picture of the item with a zoom facility that enables you to closely scrutinize the item.

Right-hand side is information about the seller.

Centre is the bidding box, and up-to-date information about this particular auction which changes as the auction progresses.

Auction Details: moving down the page you will learn more.

- Item specifics
- Description of item
- Report on condition
- Dimensions
- Cost of postage
- Shipping details
- Type of payment accepted
- Returns or no returns

Watch List

If the item is of interest, but you do not wish to place a bid, you can put it into your watch list to enable you to keep an eye on it as the auction continues.

Best Offer

In recent years eBay has given sellers a further option which perfectly captures the spirit of the antiques and collectables trade. Sellers can invite offers on an item they have listed as Buy It Now.

stunning original 1930s ART DECO Smiths sunburst clock

£195.00

This means that you might be able to buy this item for less than the Buy It Now price. Click on the Best Offer link and type in the sum that you are prepared to pay.

The seller can either accept, decline or make a counter offer. The offer lasts for 48 hours or until the auction ends.

If the seller does not respond within 48 hours the offer expires. If the offer is accepted you have been successful and are required to complete the trade. All other aspects of the auction remain the same unless it has been stated otherwise.

£195.00

Buy it now

Add to basket

Make offer

Buyers should only make an offer when they are serious about purchasing the item as, in the event of the seller accepting the offer, it is considered to be sold at the price offered.

Original 1950s telephone listed – Buy It Now £250, or Best Offer. The seller accepted an offer of £190. Both traders were totally delighted.

Bid and Pay

Look Before You Bid

With so much on offer you are bound to find something that tempts you. Having spotted something you will be eager to place a bid but you need to hold fire and do the following:

- Look at the seller's feedback.
- Check on the terms of trading.
- Discover the payment methods accepted.
- Note the cost of shipping.

Investigate the Seller's Feedback

This is the most important check you can make. You need to make sure that the feedback score and percentage are acceptable. The higher the feedback score and the closer to 100% the better. However, there are occasions when feedback is unfairly or mistakenly left by buyers and you can read the feedback comments. Fellow traders have the opportunity to reply to feedback comments left for them and sometimes the response is enough to put your mind at rest. When a wise seller receives negative feedback they do not respond with spite but in a measured tone relaying the facts.

 Has hard to find items. Ships fast from United Kingdom.

SNAP JACK 15FT ELECTRIC GUITAR CABLE/LEADIISTRAIGHT TO I ANGLE JACK PLUGS. (#262156504014)

 Fantastic transaction, all perfect. 5stars ebayer

Terms of Trading

Before placing a bid you need to check on the terms of trading. Many sellers state the time parameters by which they expect payment. Some are wary of new traders with no feedback and require you to contact them before placing a bid.

Returns Policy

Many sellers offer a returns policy to increase buyer confidence. If you are concerned about buying something you should seek out such auctions – the buyer usually pays return postage.

Cost of Shipping

What is the deal regarding shipping? This will be clearly stated in the auction details. The postage cost is made clear in the auction summary and auction page. Sellers sometimes state that buyers must collect bulky items which requires them to liaise over the arrangements.

Payment Method

Some sellers offer a range of different payment methods, others restrict it to PayPal. If you don't have a PayPal account, you need to ensure that you can comply.

Payment details

Payment method	Preferred/Accepted
PayPal VISA VISA	Accepted
Postal order/Banker's draft	Accepted
Personal cheque	Accepted

Ask Seller a Question

If you have any queries or doubts about the item or terms of the trade you should take the opportunity to contact the seller to sound them out. The link is at the bottom of the auction page. A helpful, speedy response could put your mind at rest. Select the 'Ask a question' link. The seller receives an email which is duplicated in Messages.

Ask a question

Increments

eBay auctions employ an automatic system of bid increments which become wider as the price rises. Between £1 and £5 the increment is £0.20, from £60 to £150 the increment is £5.

Proxy Bidding

This is a process for buyers whereby you leave the highest sum that you are prepared to pay for an item and leave eBay to bid on your behalf. It is automated and saves you watching the auction. You are informed by email if you win or are outbid.

How Proxy Bidding Works

Daisy has spotted a stunning vintage hat but she does not want to pay more than £35. The current bid is £15 and she is required to submit at least £15.50 to place a valid bid. However, on placing this bid the message comes back that she has been outbid, because the high bidder had placed a proxy bid.

The current bid is now £16. Daisy has to attend a meeting so decides to put in her own proxy bid of £35. She is shown as the high bidder at £24.50 (which means the other previous proxy bid was for £24). With no other buyers joining the bidding Daisy, whilst working her way up the corporate ladder, wins the hat for £24.50 (plus post and packing as stated in auction details).

Sniping

Seasoned buyers play the waiting game and place their bids in the final seconds in the hope that this will keep the price down. This holding-out mentality is prevalent on eBay so new sellers should not become despondent when their auctions continue for days with no bids. Buyers might be eagerly waiting to pounce - though this is far from certain!

Placing a Bid

Stunning Vintage Antique Country Farmh

Condition: --

Time left: **8d 07h** (10 Feb. 2016 20:21:53 GMT)

£40.00 1 bid

| 75.00| |

Submit bid

| Add to Watch list ▾ | ★ Add to collection

You want to buy this dresser and have completed the checks.
Submit your bid at the top of the auction page as shown above.
Type in the highest sum that you are prepared to pay and allow
eBay to bid on your behalf. You will only pay the minimum that
is required to win the item up to the sum you state. You will be
informed if you are outbid so you have the chance to bid again.
(As there is already a bid in place there are three possibilities –
shown below – but for the first two you can enter a higher bid.)

Bid Placed – 3 possible outcomes

•   You are immediately outbid by a proxy bid
•   Your bid did not reach reserve
•   You receive confirmation that you are the highest bidder

Make An Offer

NEW LISTING YAMAHA YTR1335 TRUMPET (

£199.00 ✒

⌐*Buy It Now*
or Best Offer
+ £20.00 postage

Some sellers state a fixed price but are open to
offers, which is made clear in the auction
results. Access the auction page where you will
discover the space where you submit your offer.
The seller will get back to you and either
accept, decline or make a counter offer.

Make offer ❓

Your offer :

£ | |

Paying for the Item

Good news – you have won the item. There is a convention of excellent service amongst eBay traders who progress their transactions in double-quick time. Paying is easy but particularly quick and convenient if you use PayPal.

Pay from My eBay

Go to My eBay – Purchase History, where you will find the auctions in which you have been successful and where those with payment outstanding are clearly flagged up.

On the right-hand side is the payment link. This takes you to the invoice page with the final price and the shipping charge. Click on Pay Now which takes you to the Review Order page which clearly sets out the details and where you select the payment method, as shown.

Pay with

⦿ **PayPal**

◯ Postal Order / banker's draft

◯ Personal cheque

Paying with PayPal

If you pay with PayPal you will cross seamlessly into your PayPal account using your password. You can select to pay from your PayPal balance or your bank account or credit card.

Paying by Cheque

To send a personal cheque locate the seller's address in Purchase History. Get it into the post as fast as you can and select 'Mark as payment sent' under More actions. The seller banks the cheque and allows the funds to clear before sending the goods - so you must be prepared to wait.

More actions ˅

Mark as payment sent

Leave Feedback

View order details

Contact seller

Thank you for your payment

Bidding on Reserve Price Auctions

Some sellers put reserves on their auctions. This means that they set a reserve price somewhere about the start price below which they are not obliged to sell. The lowest permissible reserve price is £50. The theory behind it is that they believe the, seemingly, low price tag lures the buyers in and by the time the price has risen they are too involved to walk away.

Checking the Item

When the item arrives check it straight away and ensure that it is as described. Most items are exactly as the seller stated or better. In the event of the item falling short of your expectations you should get back to the seller.

However, before you do this take a step back and consider if you are being fair and reasonable. If so, you need to carefully and calmly explain the shortfalls. With diplomacy most problems can be solved. If you are pleased with the item you should say so in feedback.

Leave Feedback

It is important that you take this last part of the transaction seriously. Sellers love receiving effusively positive feedback. You will find the link to leave feedback in Purchase History in My eBay. Click on this link to reveal the feedback form.

Rate this transaction

◉ Positive   ○ Neutral   ○ Negative   ○ I'll leave Feedback later

Tell us more

Sensational item| and speedy service - thank you.

Pictures

The Importance of Pictures

It's human nature – most eBay sales are visually driven. Pictures are a critical aspect of your auction with the power to turn browsers into buyers. They are an opportunity to show off your item – the utility, charm or special features.

Many buyers have concerns about bidding for things they cannot handle and examine. Carefully chosen pictures can put their minds at rest in a way that words never could. Even if the item you are selling is commonplace and totally standard – such as a paperback or DVD – you should include a picture.

Never stint on pictures and make sure you exploit the opportunity to the full. There are several useful ideas that you should take on board to make the most of pictures.

Cost of Basic eBay Pictures

So keen are eBay to promote the plentiful use of images that, in most instances, there is no charge for adding up to 12 standard images to eBay auctions. However, fees change on a regular basis and if you are charged for pictures it will be made clear to you before you commit to list the item.

Exploiting the Pictures

- The first (main) picture should be of the whole item
- Further pictures show it from different angles
- Include close-ups of detail and special features
- Designer labels are powerful selling points
- Makers' marks act like magnets
- Honesty pays dividends – clearly show damage and wear
- Pictures of instruction manuals reliably help the sale
- Include pictures that support claims of provenance

Shown from Every Angle

Take many pictures of the item and show it off from every angle possible. Provide clear pictures of the back and the underside, even if there is nothing much to see. Buyers need as much information as possible and multiple pictures give the impression of an open and honest seller eager to supply it.

Clever Close-Ups

Close-ups help to close the sale. This large oil painting looks impressive but a range of close-ups flaunting the rich colours and abstract detail will make it irresistible. You should include a close-up of the artist's signature.

Flaunting the Fashion

Fashion, both new and used, is huge on eBay and successfully selling it is all about the pictures.

Clothing should be:

- Modelled rather than dangling from a hanger
- Displayed without the face of the wearer
- Shown in a neutral and neat setting
- Accompanied with close ups of features or fine detail
- Shown from every angle, front, back and sides

Looking for Labels

Labels are great selling points. It goes without saying that designer labels ramp up the desirability, though labels of all kinds are a bonus. The trouble with buying clothes on eBay is that it is difficult to perceive quality from a picture. A high street label such as M&S, Next, Monsoon and Topshop give a good idea of the calibre of the garment.

Picture the Perfection – and Flaws

Sellers should carefully describe their items and accurately note missing parts, cracks and chips, flaws and general wear and tear. The documented damage to this nineteenth century mirror is so extensive that it might well deter potential buyers.

However close-ups of the damaged parts give the buyers an opportunity to weigh up the damage for themselves. Such openness and clarity speaks volumes about the integrity of the seller and their determination to make things clear.

Making the Most of Marks

Collecting is enormously popular on eBay. Some collectors exclusively buy on eBay and often from sellers they have come to trust. The appeal of a piece is enhanced by a clear picture of the maker's mark. Even if the buyer trusts that the mark is present, seeing it is a strong persuader. However it can be equally significant to a collector when a piece has no mark. Always include clear picture of the underside or back of the piece to allow the buyer to weigh it up independently.

Consider the Setting

It's not enough to include a picture, you must ensure that it enhances the auction. Only careless sellers let the world and her husband glimpse their half-eaten sandwiches and grubby draining boards with dirty dishes!

For smaller items, invest in some large sheets of A1 craft card in different colours. In this way you can ensure that lifestyle issues do not detract from the item. You can select the best shade of background to complement and show it off.

Clearly this is not feasible for larger items which should be shown off in an appropriate setting. When selling a kitchen table make sure the kitchen is clean and clutter free. Bicycles should be shown in front of a plain wall. Lawn mowers and wheelbarrows should be photographed in a spruce and tidy garden.

Turn off the Flash

Pictures are best taken without use of the flash which can leave a bright spot that mars the overall impression. You can adjust your camera setting to turn off the automatic flash.

Size and Scale

A picture is an opportunity to illustrate the size of the item. It's particularly useful when the item is surprisingly large or small. This can be done in different ways using a coin, ruler, hand or everyday item. Showing a picture indicating size is in addition to giving actual dimensions.

The Right Size of Digital Image

Recent years have seen changes in the requirements regarding the size of digital images. Up until a few years ago eBay required images to be less than 100 KB. Advances in technology mean that eBay can accommodate larger pictures. For the ideal size of picture you should adjust the size setting on your camera to 1,024 x 720 or 2,048 x 1,152 pixels. This will afford the quality required to show off the fine detail.

How to Check Image Size

Check the size of the image by resting the cursor on the picture. This reveals information about it including the file size. The optimum size is approximately 600 – 800 KB. If you have a problem loading a picture you should check the file size as it might be too large.

Item type: JPG
Date taken: 1/
Rating: Unrate
Dimensions: 1
Size: 678 KB

How To Take Perfect Pictures

- Choose a position with sufficient natural light

- Create a simple 'studio' area

- Check the camera setting

- Turn off the flash facility

- Take numerous pictures from different angles.

- Delete the non-starters and take more if required

- Upload the pictures into your eBay Selling file

- Name each file appropriately for easy recognition

Prepare to Sell

Preparing the Information

Creating an auction is simply a matter of completing the online form. For this you need details about the item as well as information gleaned from similar auctions, both current and completed. Never underestimate the value of such preparation.

Packaging

Give some thought to packaging as It is vital that fragile items are wrapped with care. Most buyers approve of recycled packaging providing it's supplied cost free. If you need to buy packaging you may find it convenient to purchase it on eBay.

Information on Postal Costs and Services

This section of the auction creation form is extremely helpful as eBay will suggest postal charges in line with the that of similar items. However, you might prefer to set your own postal charges – can search for similar items to discover the cost so that you can make yours competitive.

Get a Routine

If you plan on selling numerous items you will be surprised how much time you save by adopting a routine. Make one day your day for photography when you take, upload and prepare your eBay selling pictures. The next day is for considering the auction details and researching items. Another day could be earmarked as your listing day. Some sellers allocate shipping days, which they publish in their auction details, so that buyers know when it will be posted.

Information Required to Create Your Auction
In the order in which it is submitted:

Keywords for your item
Category (or use the suggested category)

Pictures – stored on your laptop

Item specifics – size, colour, material, make, model etc.
Details and narrative about the item
Description of condition
Auction or Fixed Price – the format you require
Start Price
Optional – Buy It Now (Fees Apply)
Optional – Reserve Price (Fees Apply)
Duration of Listing

How you will post it:
* Use eBay's recommendation
* Select your own postal method
* Buyer collect only
* Free P&P
* Local collection

International Postage
* Send to UK Shipping Centre (see page 15)
* Create your own international postal option
* No International Postage

Payment Options - how do you want to be paid?
PayPal only or state options you offer your buyer

Other Details
* Item Location
* Dispatch Time
* Returns

Optional – Auto relist if item does not sell

Researching in Completed Listings

When eBay auctions come to an end there is no further opportunity to bid or buy. However you can access them for at least a couple of weeks in completed listings. Completed auctions are invaluable for your research and often key to a successful outcome. Completed listings indicate the price you are likely to achieve. You can study every aspect of recent auctions and exploit the experience of successful sellers to your best advantage.

How to Find Completed Listings

Having undertaken a search for an item you will find the completed listings option on the left-hand side of the page. You can also choose to see just the successful auctions as these are the most informative.

Show only

☑ Completed listings
☐ Sold listings

Example of a Completed Listing

This very successful completed listing for a Victorian Penny lick (below) contains a wealth of information for anyone considering selling one. You can pick up tips from the title and details. You can also click on winning bid link (9 bids) to access the page that shows the number of bidders and how the bidding unfolded as the auction progressed. It also gives the start price, an extremely important aspect of an auction.

Victorian Tuppenny Penny Lick Two Part Moulded Glass

Item condition:	--
Ended:	22 Nov, 2015 19:06:48 GMT
Winning bid:	**£45.99** [9 bids]
Postage:	**Free** Economy Delivery
Item location:	Thatcham, United Kingdom

Choosing an Item to Sell

It is often said that you can sell anything on eBay but in reality there are restrictions. You can sell most legal and moral items but you can check on the policy in the Site Map.

Keywords

Think of the words a buyer would use to find your item. This list of keywords will form the basis of your title.

Choosing the Category

You need to get this right because some buyers eagerly browse through the category in search of their next purchase. For some items the category is obvious whilst for others it is not so easy and in recognition of this eBay offers some help. At the beginning of the auction-creating process you are required to enter keywords which brings up a list of suggested categories. Select one of these or find an alternative.

Item Specifics

These are the basic facts about the item in which there is no grey area or room for creativity. Is the wallet leather? Are the brogues size 8? Is it Gucci? Item specifics vary depending on what you are selling. The auction creation presents prompts though it is likely that not all will apply to your item. If they don't, or you are not sure, leave it blank. However, the more you can complete the better as they feature in the options on the left-hand side of the list of search results.

Condition:	**Seller refurbished** : ⓘ
Seller notes:	"Fully tested and working"
Brand:	Apple
MPN:	ME499B/A, ME499DN/A
Network:	Unlocked
Storage Capacity:	16GB

Thinking Up a Title

The collection of words that comprise your title is critical to the outcome as it is a means by which potential buyers find your item. Fortunately there is a formula for writing the optimum title:

- Think of all the possible key words
- Prioritise the keywords
- Use the first 80 characters as your title
- Arrange them to read as well as possible
- Put remaining keywords in the item description

The Title Should Include:

- Basic information. If you are selling a paperback in the book category include the words 'book' and 'paperback'.

- Model name, number and accessories are vital for modern hi-tech and electrical equipment.

- For clothes and shoes you should include the size, colour and material, whether it's for winter or summer wear and highlight an appropriate occasion.

- For home accessories include words that describe the colour (yellow brown ochre) to catch the interior designers.

The Title Should Not Include:

- Only use descriptive words such as 'lovely' if you have characters to spare – think buyer search.

Vintage Retro Style
COWBOY BOOTS
Leather Womens SIZE
UK 7 Biker Hippy
(172084453311)

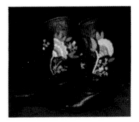

Item Description

This is your opportunity to say more about the item and pull out the stops to sell it. You should repeat the basic facts about it as well as wider details such as provenance, history, why you are selling it, what is so good about it and what you can use it for. Sound enthusiastic and make the case for buying it.

Describing Condition

One of the most exacting aspects of creating your auction is describing condition. If your item is perfect and pristine you can state this. Anything less than perfection, as in the case of the breakfast cup and saucer above, needs to be explained.

You need to look things over carefully. It's possible to own an item for years without noticing minor flaws. New does not mean perfect, so look with fresh eyes to ensure that you are not making assumptions about condition. The buyer is unable to examine the item so you must act as their eyes.

You must point out chips, cracks, flaws, tears, rubbing and wear and tear. Better still, include close-up pictures of any damage and refer to it in your description. If the damage is slight you should mention it and then dismiss it, for example:

- The small hairline crack on rim but hardly shows
- Some wear and tear that adds to the character
- Genuine wear on the base that confirms authenticity

Formula for Presenting Description

You need to inform the browsers about the item whilst giving them a reason to buy it:

- Start off enthusiastically to create the mood to buy
- Then give the facts about the item including dimensions
- Then document wear and tear, damage and flaws
- Suggest alternative uses, occasions or rooms
- Finish with a reminder of the appeal of the item

Useful expressions when describing conditions:

- In good condition for age
- A little tired
- Does not detract

Auction or Fixed Price?

This is a fundamental choice. Fixed price auctions now account for over 60% of eBay's sales but are most suitable when the price of the item is predictable. However, there are many items that are better suited to the auction process with global reach.

Auction Choices - Start Price

This is the opening price below which bids do not register. Choosing the start price is a critical to the outcome.

Advantage of a Low Start:

- Low start price attracts and excites the buyers
- Having placed a bid they anticipate owning the item

Disadvantage of Low Start:

- First bid may be the last, you are legally bound to sell

 Fortunately Rafferty chose to auction his time-ravaged die-cast Bonzo model. He was stunned when it sold for £95.

Buy It Now Price (BIN)

You can add a BIN price to the auction so that buyers can bypass the auction process and make an instant purchase.

Advantages of BIN to Seller:

- Adds urgency to an auction, bidders take action
- Sellers may receive the money sooner

Disadvantages of BIN to Seller:

- Have to consider the correct BIN
- Sellers might miss out on the power of the global market

Reserve Price

It's possible for sellers to set a reserve price (the lowest is £50) but not recommended. They are expensive and unpopular with buyers. It's better to use your start price as your reserve price.

Duration

You can choose whether you want your auction to last 1, 3, 5, 7 or 10 days. There is no difference in the cost so it depends on the nature of the item. For more substantial items a longer auction duration is advisable as buyers may need to email with questions or work out logistics such as a delivery arrangement.

Start Time

You can choose to delay the start of your auction to a time that suits you. This can be useful when you want your auction to end at a weekend or to fit in with your personal schedule.

10 out of 10 for Presentation

Many sellers make the mistake of throwing down the words without a thought to spelling and punctuation. Buyers have limited opportunities to assess the seller and the presentation of the auction is critical. Look and sound professional.

Create Your Auction

New to Selling

Most people take to buying on eBay like ducks to water but get concerned at the thought of selling. For this reason your first auction should be straightforward and you should confine your market to the UK. Remove the pound signs from your eyes and put your money-spinners to one side until you are confident, and more importantly, have earned the trust of other traders. As directed in previous chapters, prepare carefully and do your research, using completed listings if necessary.

Checklist for Selling

You have an item to sell

You have taken and stored digital pictures

You have named them appropriately

You have examined the item carefully and noted flaws

You have thought up a title containing all keywords

You have written an enthusiastic but accurate description

You have identified the category

You have considered price

Example of Creating an Auction

Item to be sold: **Victorian Penny Lick**

Start the Process

Daily Deals | Sell | Help & Contact

Click the **Sell** link at the top of the homepage to bring up the auction selling form with options tailored to suit your item.

Complete the Sell Form

The auction creation form varies depending on what you are selling. You are led through the process starting with typing in keywords that assist eBay in helping to identify the best category.

Enter Keywords to Choose a Category

Victorian Ice Cream Dish

Your keywords bring up a single category, or list of categories. You can select one of these or browse through for one that you feel best suits your item.

Select a matching category for your item:

○ Pottery, Porcelain & Glass > Glass > Art Glass > British > Bagley/ Sowerby/ Davidson

◉ Pottery, Porcelain & Glass > Glass > Date-Lined Glass > Victorian (c.1840-c.1900)

○ Pottery, Porcelain & Glass > Glass > Art Glass > Cranberry

Select another category

Create listing

Title of Keywords

Victorian Glass Penny Lick Old Ice Cream 1800s England

Adding Pictures

 Photos   Add up to 12 photos for free.

Add from computer   **Add from mobile**

Click on the link **Add from computer**. This connects with the files stored on your laptop – find your eBay Selling picture file.

Penny Lick 1   Penny Lick 2   Penny Lick Foot

:: | Penny Lick 1   ⌄ | Image Files

| Open | | Cancel |

First Picture: the Gallery Picture

Scroll through this file to locate the pictures. Make the first the main picture as it will be displayed in the auction results. Select it and click on the **Open** link. This uploads the picture and may take a couple of minutes to complete. When the picture appears, as shown, repeat the process to add more.

Main photo

Remove and Edit Pictures

To remove a picture rest the cursor on it to reveal the bin icon on the top-right. Click on this and the picture disappears. At the top-left is the link that allows you to edit the picture.

Item Specifics

Work your way through the form and select from the options you are offered – or type in your own.

Type of glass – Pressed glass

Glassware Era – Victorian (1840 - 1900)

Object type – Ice Cream Glass

Maker – Unknown

Victorian (1840-1900)

Pre-1840

Art Nouveau (1890-1914)

Art Deco (1910-1939)

1930s/ 1940s

Description

This is your opportunity to really sell your item in your own words without the constraints of a format. Give dimensions, describe condition.

A really delightful old Penny Lick
Used by street sellers to service ice cream
A penny provided a few heavenly licks.
The glass is chunky pressed glass
Stands 3 1/4 inches - 8.5 cms high
Shows all the signs of authentic hand made
With striations and air bubbles and flaws
The base of the foot has a gadget mark

Auction Format and Start Price

Auction-style listings are best when you're not sure how much your item could sell for.

Fixed-price listings are best when you know how much you want to get.

| Auction | Fixed price |

£0.99 recommended > £ 9.90

Auction or **Fixed Price** - select your choice.

Start Price - The suggested start price of 99p (based on previous sales) has not been taken up. The start price of £9.90 was chosen for this auction (based on personal experience).

Buy It Now Price (Can be added to auction - fee charged).

Reserve Price (Fee charged and not generally recommended).

Listing duration - 1, 3, 5, 7 or 10 days?

Schedule a start time - to suit you and your potential market.

How You'll Post It

Select postage for me   Select postage myself   Offer local collection only

You have three choices: accept the postal method and cost recommended, choose your own, or state your buyer collects. Click on the tab to reveal the appropriate screen.

In this example the recommended postage is accepted:

2nd class Royal Mail, 2 - 3 working days for £2.80

International Postage

International postage (optional) ℹ️

○ Send your package to the UK Shipping Centre and the rest will be taken ca

○ Create your own international postage option

◉ No international postage

See page 15 for an explanation of the Global Postage scheme. Not all items or all sellers are eligible. In this auction this option has not been selected and the sale is confined to the UK.

Review Your Preferences

This includes the payment methods that you accept, the location of the item (needs to be updated if there are any changes). You must state your despatch time so that buyers, who are often making time-critical purchases, know when they can expect to receive the item. You also need to consider your returns policy.

At the end of the creation process you have three options:

Preview it

Save as draft

List it

Congratulations sale.

Here's your listing on eBay:
Victorian Glass Penny Lick Old I

What's next:
- If you need to make changes

Item Specifics Alternatives

Item specifics are tailored for each item. The best auctions provide all possible information.

Antique armchair auctions can be enhanced with information on the type, age and material used with options from beech to walnut.

Shoe auctions encourage sellers to to offer extensive detail including the height and type of heel – Cuban, stiletto, kitten and wedge.

Many items, including gadgets and home appliances have identification serial numbers that can be submitted to bring up standard information and images on the particular model.

Laptops & Electronics

Entering **Acer Laptop** brings up a range of models with links to comprehensive information on each. It makes light work of listing such items though you need to document your item's condition.

Books & DVDs

You can access useful standard information on books and DVDs by typing the titles into the sell search facility and looking through the list of options that appear. Click on the appropriate link.

Watch Your Auction

Live Auction Action

Your auction is live - the countdown has begun. You can make a significant difference to the outcome (whether or not your item sells and the price achieved) with careful tending. You should be prepared to:

• Speedily answer questions from potential buyers

• Assess the response to your auction

• Revise your auction if necessary

Answer Questions

eBay contact you by email when a buyer sends you a question and, as with all significant communications, this is duplicated in My eBay - Messages. Welcome questions as they are an opportunity to start a dialogue with your potential buyers. Go to: **Messages – My eBay** and use the link provided to respond.

Assess Your Auction

An eBay auction is unlike a local auction in that it runs for a specified length of time, rather than until the final bid. Typically eBay buyers wait until the last minutes (or nail-biting final seconds) of an auction to place their bids (in an attempt to keep the price down). This makes it hard to assess the likely outcome, though amongst the useful indications of interest are the number of visitors and watchers.

My eBay

Watch your auction (and when the time comes progress the transaction) in My eBay. On the left-hand side of My eBay is the summary of your selling activities. Your live auctions are listed in **Active**. In the example on the right there are two ongoing auctions. Use the link to view the auction summaries.

Sell

All selling

Sell an item

Saved drafts (20)

Scheduled (0)

Active (2)

Sold (3)

Unsold (2)

Active Auction Summary

Views/Watchers	Bids	Price	Time left ▲	Actions
20	1	£9.90	5d 01h	Sell similar
7				More actions ▼

This summary gives useful details such as the number of views (20) and watchers (7). The price turns from red to green when a bid has been placed indicating that the item will certainly sell, though the wait is on to learn at what price. The summary also gives the user ID of the high bidder. There are links on the right-hand side - including **More actions**.

Page Views

A useful indicator of the interest in your auction is the number of page views, which are calculated by a smart counter that records unique visits. This means, if you look at an item 20 times from the same laptop the number of visits will be noted as 1. In terms of a successful outcome the more views the better, and certainly no views would result in no sale.

Watchers

Buyers put items that interest them in their **Watch list**. The seller is informed of the number of watchers but not their user IDs. In the example above there are 7 watchers (with 5 days to go). This does not mean that they will bid (they might be doing research) but it indicates the level of interest.

Access the Auction Page Through the Title

Victorian Glass Penny Lick Old
Ice Cream 1800s Eng... (20151:

Each live auction summary is listed with the gallery picture, beside which is the auction title (as shown above). Click on the auction title to access the live auction page.

Live Auction Page

Victorian Glass Penny Lick

Condition: --

Time left: **3d 06h** (03 Feb, 2016 16:3

£12.50 3 bids

The auction page captures the action as it unfolds and duplicates the view other users enjoy but with some additional features. This includes the current price, the bidding, and the countdown. There are also links at the top of this page to assist sellers, including the Revise your item link to allow you to make changes to the auction, if required (shown on Page 84).

Bids Link

The live auction page shows the current price of the item and the number of bids received so far. This is a link whereby you can access the Bid History page which shows how the bidding is unfolding with their User IDs and feedback. The greater number of bidders the better, though many buyers keep a low profile until the final seconds.

Check the Bidders

Occasionally bids need to be cancelled. You are permitted to cancel bids on your auction in certain circumstances. It might be that there is a mishap with the item you are selling or you are not satisfied about the track record of the trader.

Revising a Live Auction

Revise your item lets you add information to the description
or upload additional pictures. You can add pictures at any
time but you can only change an item description if no bids
have been placed and there are more than 12 hours left.
There are some things that cannot be changed, for example:
Auction-style listings cannot be changed to Fixed Price listings.

Rules Regarding Revising Live Auctions

To find all the rules that concern changing live auctions go to:
**Help – Selling & seller fees – Managing your selling activity
– Revising single listing on eBay**

How to Revise Your Auction

Revise your item

Sell a similar item

Create postage discounts

Locate the auction page via the Active sell link in My eBay.
Click on the title to reach the live auction page. At the top of this
page are the links as shown above. Revise your item returns
you to the original auction form where you can use the edit link.
This also where you come to add or remove pictures in the
same way that you originally uploaded them.

Additional Pictures

If a potential buyer contacts you with questions about an aspect
of the item – a point of detail or the nature of a flaw – you may
decide to post an additional picture to address their concerns
and to provide clarity.

When you have made all the
desired changes you can either
Preview them or click on the
Revise it link as shown.

Preview

Your Item Has Sold

If you haven't watched the end of your auction you will receive an email from eBay informing you that your item has sold.
Go to **My eBay – Sold** to access the auction summary.

Sold Link in My eBay

This reveals the list of successful auction summaries. On the right-hand side of each summary are the links to progress your transaction. Amongst them you will find a link to send your buyer an invoice though some buyers are quick off the mark and send the money via PayPal immediately.

More actions ▼

Print postage label

Add tracking number

View order details

View PayPal transaction

Contact buyer

Mark as not dispatched

Unmark as payment received

Second Chance Offer

It is not unheard of for a buyer to 'vanish'. eBay have responded to this problem by devising a system called the **Second Chance Offer** whereby the item can be offered to an under bidder at the price of their bid. You can find the list of bidders and sums they bid via the **Bid History** link on the auction page in **My eBay - Sold**.

Sellers should always try to resolve things with the high bidder first and eBay will contact the winning bidder on your behalf. However, if the high bidder disappears, or you agree amicably between you to cancel the transaction, Second Chance Offer is a good compromise.

Beware of Outside Offers

Occasionally buyers request that you stop the auction mid-sale and sell to them privately. Or, if the item fails to sell, they ask you to accept an outside offer. This kind of deal should be politely declined as you will not be protected by eBay's seller protection and it goes against eBay's rules.

Your Buyer's Address

You will find your buyer's address in **My eBay - Sold** through the links on the auction page. Do not send the item until you have received payment. If your buyer pays by cheque you should wait until the funds clear.

Packing the Item

After all the preparation and activity you need to get this right. Some items are enhanced by the use of coloured tissue paper, which is luxurious but affordable. For fragile goods there is no such thing as too much bubble wrap and no one minds if it's recycled. Most postal insurances cover loss but not breakage.

Postal Insurance & Proof of Posting

Expensive items should be insured but for low value items it might not be worth the outlay as the standard postal service includes some insurance. For a parcel travelling within the United Kingdom consider sending it 'Special Delivery' or 'Signed For' as they are low cost and require a signature. Whatever you decide it's essential to get proof of posting.

Friendly Note

Include a friendly note to the buyer. Thank them for their custom and remind them of your returns policy if you have one.

Relist Your Item

Not everything sells but you can comfort yourself with the thought that the cost of failing to sell on eBay is low – and for the first 20 items entirely free. To find the link to relist your item go to: **My eBay – Unsold.** Take the opportunity to consider why it didn't sell and edit your auction to make it more tempting to the buyers to increase your chance of success.

Feedback

Even though feedback for buyers is limited, you should say something friendly that reflects their good practice. Buyers return to sellers that they like.

eBay App

The Case for the App

There was a time when harassed traders rushed home to log on so they could check on their auctions. All this has changed with the introduction of the eBay App – a program that operates on your smartphone or tablet, and allows you to progress your eBay trading. It's an extension of your eBay account and contains all the information you require to manage your auctions, whilst you are on the move or in the comfort of your own home. The App is easy to understand, simple to use and incorporates PayPal. It's a quantum leap in convenience – you just need to familiarise yourself with the layout and functions.

How to Download the eBay App - see page 42

Layout of the App

≡   Q Search eBay   🛒

Activity   Shop   Sell
                _____

egories   **Featured**   Fashio

Similar to eBay's homepage on desktop, the opening screen of the eBay App consists of links. They are as follows:

At the top of the screen:
Menu symbol – Search eBay – Basket symbol

Further down the screen are the main links:
Activity – Shop – Sell

Towards the bottom of the screen are:
Categories – Featured – Fashion

App Menu

≡   Q Search eBay   🛒

At the top of the screen on the left-hand side is the menu icon. Tap this to reveal your Messages and Notifications – explained on page 90. Beneath those are the following links:

Home – Watching – Buying – Selling – Following

Tap on each to reveal:

Home – takes you to the opening screen as shown above.

Watching – the auctions you have placed in your watch list.

Buying – stores all your buying-related activities. It lists your recent purchases and the status of the transaction, whether it is awaiting payment, paid for or already dispatched. It also shows the items that you didn't win.

Selling - contains a link to start the selling process, lists the drafts of auctions awaiting completion, items you have sold and items that failed to sell with a relist link.

Following – comprises your followed searches and sellers.

Messages

Notifications

Home

Watching

Buying

Selling

Following

Help & Contact   Settings

Search eBay

Type keywords here and tap the search icon to display a list of relevant auctions. You can find items to buy immediately, or add to your watch list for future consideration.

≡   Q gripping thriller paperback   🛒

Activity

Tap on the **Activity** link to view:
Recently viewed items and watched items.
Buying Overview - consisting Bids, Offers and Purchases
Selling Overview - consisting Sold, unsold, following

Shop

This main link consists of:
Featured Deals, Featured Sales & Events

Sell

Cash it in - sell something today - the link to instigating the selling process. It includes Drafts and Unsold.

Basket

When you wish to buy multiple items you can put them into the basket and pay in one PayPal transaction, including to different sellers. The number icon shows how many items it contains.

Messages

This duplicates Messages in My eBay and contains all your correspondence from eBay and other users. You can respond to a message by tapping it and following the links.

Notifications

Notifications acts as a reminder of latest developments and outstanding tasks that need progressing.

Help and Contact

This is the section you will come to in the event that something goes wrong. There are several links to assist you including:

•   Returning an item
•   Didn't receive your item

Settings

This contains some of the information held in the Account section of My eBay including: Delivery Address, change password and notifications.

Notifications in settings contains:

• Buying notifications
• Selling notifications
• General notifications
• Customise sounds – including quiet times

Overview of Buying Using the App

- Undertake a keyword search

- Or tap on 'categories' to browse the possibilities

- Use the **Refine** link at top of screen to hone search

- Use the **Sort** option at top of screen to organise results

- Scroll through the list of auction results

- Tap on the title of auction that interests you to access the auction page

- The auction page shows pictures, details of item and ongoing auction as it unfolds

- Scroll across to view all the pictures - indicated by arrows

- Scroll down for information of item and auction terms

- Either add to **Watch List** or return to **Search Results**

- Or use links at bottom of screen to **Buy It Now** or **Bid**

- Pay for BIN item using your PayPal account via link

- Follow the progress of the bidding in **Activity**

- On winning an item with successful bid pay using links

- Leave feedback using links in **Activity** - **Purchases**

Example of Using the App to Buy

Using the Search box at top of screen, type in
'Portable Radio' – it brings up 685 items from all categories

Refine

Use **Refine** option to exclude items from the search results that are not of interest. The choices in Refine include:

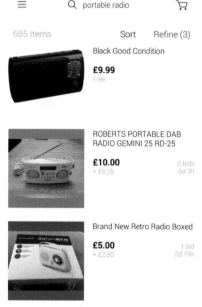

≡   Q portable radio   🛒

685 Items   Sort   Refine (3)

Black Good Condition
£9.99
Free

ROBERTS PORTABLE DAB
RADIO GEMINI 25 RD-25
£10.00   0 bids
+ £6.25   6d 3h

Brand New Retro Radio Boxed
£5.00   1 bid
+ £2.80   2d 19h

Category
Buying format
Condition
Price range
Distance from you
Delivery options
(including free delivery)
Completed listings

In this example Auction Format and Condition / New were selected.

Sort

Use **Sort** to control the order in which the auction results are presented. The options include:

Lowest Price + Postage – presents with the lowest price first
Highest Price + Postage – presents with highest price first
Ending Soonest – enables you to easily limit the wait
Newly Listed – most recently listed items
Nearest First – items closest to your appear first

Scroll through the auction results. Each picture and auction summary gives an idea of the item on offer. When you find something of interest tap on the title to enter the auction page.

Auction Page

The auction page should have the information needed to assess an item but if you have any questions you can contact the seller. The auction page indicates the current status of the live auction:

Vintage Radio

Auction with 1 bid – current price £5.

Postage is £5.50 and estimated delivery date stated.

Item Description – enthusiastic, informative and includes:

FM, LW & MW bands. Pull out extendable aerial and carrying handle. Sounds great and works on both mains (lead supplied) or batteries (not supplied).

Condition

The radio is in used, generally good, condition, but not perfect and the flaws are carefully explained.

Returns

With no returns on this item it is important to tap the link which gives the track record of the seller.

About the Seller - feedback score is (78) 100% positive.

Bid for the item by using the link at bottom-right of the screen.

	1 mth	6 mths	12 mths
Positive	6	33	79
Neutral	0	0	0
Negative	0	0	0

Watch	Place bid

Placing a Bid

Tap the Place Bid link to bring up the box and enter your bid. Submit the most that you are prepared to pay for it, safe in the knowledge that eBay only uses the sum required to win the item, up to your maximum.

We'll bid for you, up to

£6.50

You can use the keyboard to type in your own bid (£6.50 as shown). Or you can tap on the suggested sums just above the keyboard (£6, £7 or £10). You will be informed if you are winning but if other bidders join the fray you will receive a message from eBay if you are outbid.

You are the High Bidder – So Far!

Follow the auction progress in **Activity – Buying** by tapping on the menu symbol on the top left-hand side of the screen. This reveals the list that includes the Buying option. Tap this to show the ongoing auction summary indicating that you are currently winning. Tap onto it to access the live auction page and view the details.

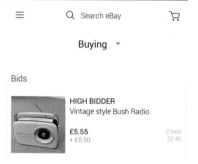

You have been Outbid

If you are outbid (which is clearly indicated) as was the case in this auction, you can use the link to return and place a higher bid. Second time round, and determined to succeed, a bid was submitted for £30, the highest sum the buyer was prepared to pay (though hoping to win it for less!)

You Have Won

Good news – you have won the item! If you haven't been watching the auction you will be informed by email which is duplicated in Messages. You will now find this transaction with the links to progress it in:

Congratulations, you've won this auction, please pay now

£26.50 + £5.50 postage

Sale date   5 Jan 2016 21:40

Pay now

Contact the seller

Leave Feedback

Activity - Buying - Purchases.

How to Pay

Paying for it is easily and speedily done using your PayPal account which is integrated into the App.

<   Pay with PayPal

Log In   **PayPal** 🔒

Access your Activity section, as shown in previous page. Go to Purchases and find the portable radio transaction. Enter the completed auction by tapping the title. As the illustration shows you will find the links to paying for the item.

Leaving Feedback

In most instances buyers are delighted with their purchase. You need to reflect this satisfaction in feedback. The links to leaving feedback are in **Activity - Purchases**. Go into the completed auction where you will discover the link for leaving feedback - shown above. Say something that reflects the trade and remember, more is more when it comes to praise on eBay.

PAID
Vintage style Bush Radio

£26.50
+ £5.50

Overview of Selling Using the App

- Select **Sell** link from home screen

- Tap on **Sell something today**

- Enter title / keywords to bring up suggested categories

- Select a suggested categories (or decide on your own)

- **Sell an Item** screen appears with list of requirements

- Select the **Photos** link

- From the Photos screen tap on camera icon to start process of adding pictures. (See page 98)

- When finished adding pictures tap on arrow icon at top

- Tap on **Description** link and complete details

- Tap on **Format & Price** and submit requested details

- Tap on **Postage** link and supply details

- Tap on **Preferences** to state Returns policy

- Either **Save** for later or **Continue**

- Check through the details in the **Review** screen

- Either – **Preview** your auction to see how it will look

- Or – List with displayed fees

Example of Using the App to Sell

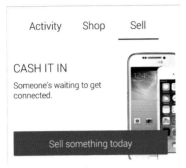

Selling men's socks: first check that you have suitable pictures stored on your mobile phone.

From the home screen of the App select **Sell** from the top options as shown above.

This takes you into the Sell an item auction creation screen as shown below.

Title

Type in keywords which are the basis of a title which allows the app to suggest one (or more) categories.

Choosing a Category

Read through the list of categories and select the most appropriate. As the illustration shows two sections – Title and Categories – are now completed.

Photos Link

Tap on the Photos link at the top of the list to add pictures to your auction. There is a step-by-step guide on the next page.

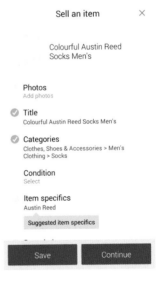

Save as Draft

When you have completed each section tap on the arrow symbol (shown) at the top of the screen to move to the next stage. If at any point you run out of time you can use the **Save** link to save the details in drafts.

Step-by-Step Adding Pictures to Your Auction

In my long experience of teaching eBay trading, adding pictures is the part that most concerns new traders the most. In fact it's straightforward on the site – but even simpler using the App! If you do have difficulties with any aspect of creating your auction there are links to seek help and assistance.

Step 1 – Tap the camera symbol to reveal the options – new photo or gallery.

Step 2 – Select gallery to connect to the pictures that are stored in the gallery of your mobile phone.

Step 3 – By tapping the gallery symbol you will access your pictures. You need to select the main picture first as this is the one that appears with the auction search results and should represent the item as a whole.

Step 4 – The picture appears with the edit option to rotate or crop. Use the link at the bottom of the screen to upload pictures. It might take a minute or two for it to upload.

Step 5 – The picture has successfully uploaded – the first picture is in place. To add more pictures to your auction use the camera symbol and repeat the process.

Step 6 – This picture appears sideways and needs rotating. Use the Rotate link at the bottom of the screen to turn it to present it the right way up.

Step 7 – The second picture has been successfully rotated and uploaded. You can add up to 12 standard pictures for free.

Step 8 – When you have added all the pictures you want to display, tap the arrow link at the top of the screen to move to the next phase.

Step 1

Step 2

Step 3

Step 4

Step 5

Step 6

Step 7

Step 8

Condition Choices

Choices are:
New with tags, New without tags, New with defects or Used.
Any defects need to be explained in item description.
The socks are – **New with tags**

Item Specifics

These involve the basics about the item that rule it in or out -
such as size and colour. It can include the make, model and
identification numbers. The specifics vary according to the item
concerned. In this simple example they consist:

One size – Regular
Brand – Austin Reed
Main colour – Multi
Style – Snazzy and confident (personally tailored description)
Specifics also include material and garment care etc

Item Description

This is your opportunity to sell your item in your own words.
However, your sales patter must be realistic so as not to cause
disappointment to your buyer.

'You can tell all you need to know of a man from his socks'

Enthusiastic but realistic with special attention to condition.

Format and Price

You have several options for type of sale – Auction, Fixed Price
(Buy It Now), Auction with BIN, Fixed Price with Best Offer.

Additional choices:

Reserve (Not recommended and incurs a fee)
Duration – 7 days
Start time – choose the time your auction goes live.

Postage

You can use eBay's recommended postal charges based on the average charges for similar items. Otherwise you can state your own providing you are clear about the service your buyer is getting for their money with an estimated delivery date.

- Offer free postage
- Offer collection in person
- Add additional postal options
- Use eBay's Global Shipping Programme

Preferences

How do you want to be paid?
You have to offer your buyers PayPal but you are free to give them additional alternatives as shown.

Make your choices by selecting the box and then tapping on OK.

Payment methods	
Personal cheque	☐
Money order/Cashier's check	☐
See description	☐
Escrow	☐
Credit card	☐
CANCEL	OK

Handling Time and Item Location

You need to give your buyers an idea of when they can expect to receive the item should they win it. The item location is important when the item requires collection by the buyer.

Returns Policy

Your basis choices are:
Returns accepted
No returns accepted

If returns are accepted you need to state the terms such as, within what time frame can an item be returned and who pays the return postage.
Tap continue to proceed.

Preview Your Listing

Take the opportunity to see how it looks to buyers. Scrutinise it with critical eyes to ensure it gives the best possible impression. Click on the link to list your item.

Activity – Selling

Keep in touch with your auction in this section. You can see how many visitors your auction has attracted and how many have put it on their watch list. You many be contacted with questions which will appear in **Messages** and can be answered using the link. You can easily make changes to the ongoing auction using the **Revise listing** link.

Revise listing

End listing

Sell similar item

1 of 2

Sold

Sellers receive the money before sending the item. When you receive payment via PayPal this is indicated in **Activity – Sold** Once payment is secured you need to act quickly and in line with your stated dispatch time. You find the buyer's address in Activity – Sold.

Activity - Sold

Use the links in this section to complete the transaction, including leaving feedback, and to show your buyer:

- Item dispatched
- Feedback left

Relist Item

Use the links in **Activity – Selling – Unsold** to relist the item. You can take the opportunity at this point to make changes to increase the chances of it selling second time round.

eBay Fees

Most Current Information

There have been many changes regarding fees over the years and the most reliably current information is the site itself. The link is **Site Map – Selling Resources – eBay.co.uk Fees.**

Cost of Selling on eBay

Buying is free on eBay but sellers are charged a fee. (Charges include VAT at current rate.) The fee is composed of 3 parts:

- Listing Fee – this is non-refundable (subject to offer and does not always apply)
- Final Value Fee – based on the price achieved
- Postage Fee – based on the postal charge

Listing Fee

The listing fee is comprised of the insertion fee plus any extra selling enhancements you choose to take advantage of, such as enhanced pictures, scheduled listing etc. This fee is charged regardless of whether or not the item sells. However, currently there are no insertion fees for the first 20 listings every month.

Understanding eBay Charges to Sellers

Listing Fee (when it applies) + Final Value Fee + Postal Charges Fee = eBay Fees
Listing Fee = Insertion + Selling Enhancements
Final Value Fee = 10% of winning bid up to £75
Postal Charges Fee = 10% of postal charges
Car, Property & Media differ and should be checked on site

eBay's Current Fees – Free to List

YOUR SELLING FEES

There are no insertion fees for your first 20 listings every month. Each month you can create 20 listings for free in either Auction or Buy It Now formats with the following exceptions:

- Motors category is not included
- Classified Ads is not included
- Subject to some selling limits for new sellers
- Subject to limits if your feedback score reflects you have fallen below standard

Final Value Fee

Your final value fee is 10% of your total transaction (price achieved plus postage charged as shown below).

- You only pay a final value fee if your item sells
- You never pay more than £250 as a final value fee
- If your buyer pays with PayPal, you will pay PayPal fees

When the Final Value Fee Applies

Final value is the last bid, doesn't apply if item receives no bids. Final Value Fee does not apply if item fails to reach the reserve. Final Value Fee on Buy It Now auctions is the Buy It Now price.

Relisting Fee

If an item fails to sell the seller is encouraged to list it again. When you relist an item it counts towards your 20 free listings.

Final Value Fee on Postal Charges

Sellers are also charged 10% of the shipping charges which are shown in My eBay – Account – see example below

Item	Fee type	Amount (GBP)
201459476947	Final Value Fee	**£1.70**
201459476947	Final Value Fee on Shipping	**£0.28**

Examples of eBay's Fees + PayPal Fees

PayPal fees only apply when buyer pays using PayPal.

Nikon Digital Camera

High Bid – £140
Postage – £3.30
Final Value Fee – £14
Fee on Postage – £0.33
eBay Charges – £14.33

PayPal Fees
Buyer Sends – £143.30
PayPal Charges – £5.07
Total Charges to Seller – £19.40

Vintage Japanese Tile

High Bid – £16
Postage – Free
Final Value Fee – £1.60
eBay Charges – £1.60

PayPal Fees
Buyer Sends – £16
PayPal Charges – £0.74
Total Charges to Seller – £2.34

Cost of Optional Auction Enhancements

You can boost the appeal of your auction with some enhancements, though they are entirely optional and much depends on what you are selling. The fees are per listing.

Gallery Plus   £2.50
Shows larger pictures in search results

Buy It Now (BIN)   £0.50
You can add a BIN price to your auction-style listings. When a bid is placed this disappears.

Subtitle
Add a subtitle to your auction   £1.00

Listings Designer   £0.30
Add a design template to your listings
(Available only in Advanced Listing)

List in Two Categories   Doubles Listing Fee
Items appear in two categories. Useful when there is more than one ideal category.

Scheduler   20 per month free
Decide when your listing goes live   After that £0.06p

Special offers

Selling on eBay is rendered more lucrative by the special offers that regularly appear. Some concern a particular weekend, an entire week or a quota of free listings per month. They make selling on eBay irresistible!

Reviewing Fees

At the end of the auction creation process, just before you submit it, you see breakdown of charges. It's an opportunity to weigh up your choices and make appropriate amendments.

Fees – Selling For Charity

Charitable giving is wholeheartedly supported by eBay who make it as easy as possible to give to good causes. You can donate up to 100% of your item's final sale price to an eBay registered charity. In this event eBay return to you the same percentage of your selling fees (excluding fees for optional listing upgrades).

Checking Your Account

You can check your eBay charges at any time. Select the Account link in My eBay.

Click on the Seller Account link to view the charges.

You can choose how you want to pay eBay charges and use this link to make any changes to these arrangements.

All administrative matters are located in the Account section of My eBay.

Understanding Your eBay Seller's Account

Once inside your eBay seller account you can check on all fees. You can view your most recent invoices up to four months ago.

Fee Type	Amount*	Balance
Final Value Fee	£11.19	£29.98
Final Value Fee	£0.90	£30.88
Gallery Fee	--	£30.88
Insertion Fee	£0.15	£31.03

Your invoices show the detail of all your selling activity. eBay give the running total of your charges.

Change Your Account Details

It's very easy to change your details. My eBay is a good start point for all such changes. Go to My eBay - Account.
The Personal Information and Addresses links allow you to keep your details current. The Preferences options allows you to tailor the notifications you receive from eBay to suit your exact requirements.

My Account
- Personal Informatio
- Addresses
- Notification Preferer
- Site Preferences
- Seller Dashboard
- Feedback
- PayPal Account
- Seller Account

User ID and Passw

Account type

User ID

Password

Secret question

About Me page

Change Your Password

Use this link to change your password. The secret question allows you to identify yourself to eBay in the event of forgetting your password.

About Me page is your chance to promote confidence and connect with your buyers. It's your chance to air your enthusiasm, experience and expertise in the things you are selling.

Safety, Security, Q & A's

Pro-active Safety and Security

The vast majority of eBay's millions of members are trustworthy and keen to promote honest trading. Unfortunately there are a small number of crooks that see eBay as a golden opportunity, and attempt to trick unsuspecting traders into parting with money or private details to rob them. However, in the same way that you can protect yourself from theft in your everyday life, you can incorporate routine security measures into your online activities. The following will help keep you safe from fraud:

- eBay Toolbar

- PayPal

- Messages

- Password

- Log Out

- Safety Centre

eBay Toolbar

The Toolbar enables you to keep an eye on things even when you are not on the eBay site. You can receive alerts and view your buying and selling status from your desktop.

PayPal Security for Sellers

There are many advantages to using PayPal (discussed in Chapter 4) including security. You don't have to give out sensitive details – address, credit card number or bank account information – to strangers and it incorporates guarantees.

Messages – Spoofs

These are emails that appear to be from eBay but are an attempt by crooks to get your personal details to rob you. Spoofs usually claim that something is amiss and often threaten to suspend your account unless you react immediately. Go to to **My eBay - Messages.** If it's not duplicated there, it's not from eBay. The email should be forwarded to spoof@ebay.com for investigation.

Messages – Pharming

Some spoof emails direct you to a fake website where they request you sign in with your user ID and password. These fake sites look convincing but the URL (web address) at the top of the page is not a genuine eBay URL. Go to **My eBay - Messages** to see if it's there. If not, forward it for investigation, as above.

Passwords

Your password must be obscure and private and solely for your eBay trading.

Log Out

When you have completed your session you should log out.

Safety Centre

Security on eBay is constantly being enhanced and you can keep up to date with the changes through the Safety Centre.

Problems and Solutions

Seller Mistake – Lalique Perfume Bottle

I have just sold a Lalique Perfume Bottle to a collector who paid by PayPal. I described it as perfect not realising it has a small chip. My buyer loves it but is disappointed, what should I do?

ANSWER We all make mistakes and to your credit you have fallen on your sword. Apologise profusely and ask her what she would like to do. Make it clear that her satisfaction is your main concern and if she wants a refund you will pay return postage. However, you could suggest a monetary adjustment which is easily done through PayPal links. If she likes this idea ask what sum returned to her would make her happy.

Gone Girl Buyer – Occasional Table

I've just sold a glass-topped occasional table but the buyer has disappeared. It's annoying as there were several bidders and it went for a good price but now I cannot get a response from her.

ANSWER It's possible that she is daunted by the prospect of having to pick it up. Some people get carried away and forget to factor in these practicalities. Be kind. Send your high bidder a friendly message saying that you are prepared to void the transaction – the link is in My eBay – Sold. Then contact an under bidder and make them a Second Chance Offer whereby, if they accept, they purchase the item at the cost of their bid.

Problem With Pictures

I was getting on very nicely with my eBay selling and have sold several items. However, since my son-in-law used my camera I have been unable to upload pictures to my auctions. I click the upload link and the icon just continues to spin!

ANSWER It's possible that he changed the setting on your camera to large or very large. Check the size setting on your camera and adjust it back to medium, then try again (see p66).

Blocking a Buyer

I had a bad experience with a buyer who ended up insulting me. It has upset me and put me off trading on eBay.

ANSWER This is bad luck but rare. I doubt that this individual will bother you again but go to **Site Map - Manage Bidders** and block them by entering their user ID, for reassurance.

Research in Completed Listings

I'm new to selling and I have loads of collectable items to sell but have no idea what they are worth or how to describe them.

Show only

☐ Completed listings
☐ Sold listings

ANSWER Research items in Completed listings. Undertake a keyword search, then use the options on the left hand side to bring up the completed listings. Scroll through until you find a similar item that was successfully sold and study the details.

Buying a Laptop

I want to buy a laptop but am concerned that it will go wrong.

For this item, the seller provides:
eBay Premium Service

ANSWER Seek out an eBay recommended seller. These are professional sellers guaranteed to give you a great service.

Terms Explained

About Me

Create a page that tells other members all about
you. It promotes credibility and trust.

Announcement Board

Where eBay tells the community about changes to the site.

Auction Buy It Now

An auction with a Buy It Now option. The Buy It Now option
disappears when the first bid is placed.

Best Offer

This is an option for sellers of Buy It Now items that allows
traders to negotiate the exact price. The seller can accept,
decline or counter offer. Look for the Submit a Best Offer link.

Bid Cancellation

This is an action taken by a seller during a live auction. It is rare
but happens when something is amiss. Possibly the item has
been broken or the seller is not happy about the bidder.

Bid Increments

The steps by which the bids increase. They automatically widen
as the price of the item rises.

Bid Retraction

This happens where a member withdraws their bid on an item.
There are limited circumstances when this is allowed.

Browsing

Finding items to buy by looking through the categories and sub-
categories.

Buy It Now

An item can be listed as a Buy It Now or as an auction with a Buy It Now option to facilitate immediate purchase.

Completed Search

This is a search for an item that has been listed and the auction is finished. You cannot bid but it's useful for research.

eBay Explained

This section provides all the answers. It's conveniently organised by topic with FAQs (frequently asked questions) but also contains a link to contact customer services.

eBay Stores

The success of the site has encouraged its broader evolution. By opening up a shop eBay sellers can capitalise on their success.

eBay Toolbar

A free download toolbar with potential security feature that offers easy access to eBay and helps keep track of items.

Escrow

A third party is paid a small fee to hold the buyer's money until they signify they are happy with the item. Used for costly items.

Final Value Fee

The part of the fee charged to the seller when an item is sold.

Fixed Price

The Buy It Now price where there is no bidding and buyers can purchase immediately.

Global Shipping Programme (GSP)

A scheme whereby you send your successfully sold items to a UK address – international postage and customs and paperwork (where it applies) is handled for you.

Insertion Fee

The non-refundable fee charged for listing an item in an auction.

Keyword

A word put into the search engine to find a particular item.

Keyword Spamming

The practice of using irrelevant words in an auction listing to attract more attention though the keyword search.

My eBay

Your own personal space on the site where you find details of all your activities including buying and selling and seller's account. It's also where you find the links to progress your trading.

Messages

A security innovation to eliminate fraudulent spoof emails. Authentic messages are duplicated in My Messages.

Navigation Bar

The links at the top of a page that enable you to move around the site.

Negative Feedback

An unfavourable report left for a seller by a buyer that detracts from the seller's feedback score and percentage.

Neutral Feedback

A report by a buyer on a seller that is not positive or negative but which is considered to be a black mark.

Positive Feedback

A favourable report on a trader by a buyer or seller which adds a point to their feedback score.

Premium Seller

Active seller who agrees to operate within particular high standards of trading and retain at least 98% positive feedback.

Private Auction

An auction where the User IDs of bidders are not displayed.

Proxy Bidding

Allows bidders to put in the highest sum they would pay for an item and leave the system to automatically bid for them.

Relisting

Using the links to relist an item that did not sell first time round.

Reserve Price

A price that is higher than the start price but the lowest sum acceptable to the seller. The lowest reserve permissible is £50.

Scheduled Listing

Delaying the start of an auction to a time that suits the seller. This is usually to optimise the time the auction ends.

Second Chance Offer

In the event of the high bidder pulling out the item can be offered to a non-winning bidder with the eBay fees adjusted accordingly.

Shill Bidding

This refers to the illegal placing of bids to artificially raise the price of an item.

Sniping

Placing a bid in the final minutes or seconds of the auction. Delayed bidding tends to be the norm on eBay.

Start Price

The opening price for the item in an auction below which bids are not registered. It is determined by the seller though eBay will make suggestions based on successful auctions.

Under Bidder

The highest bidder beneath the winner who, in the event of the buyer not following through, could be offered the item.

Watch List

A buyer can place items that interest them into their Watch List which is accessed in My eBay.

Index